Credo

by
Edmund Banyard

ISBN 0 85346 226 7
© The United Reformed Church, 2004

by Edmund Banyard

Published by Granary Press
the imprint of The United Reformed Church
86 Tavistock Place, London WC1H 9RT

All rights reserved. No part of this publication may be reproduced in any form or by any means – graphic, electronic, or mechanical, including photocopying, recording, taping or information storage and retrieval systems – without the prior permisssion in writing of the publishers.

The publishers make no representation, express or implied, with regard to the accuracy of the information contained in this book and cannot accept any legal responsibility for any errors or omissions that may take place.

Produced by Communications and Editorial, Graphics Office

Printed by Healeys Printers, Unit 10, The Sterling Complex,
Farthing Road, Ipswich, Suffolk IP1 5AP

Contents

Introduction   1

Chapter

1   **BEYOND ALL KNOWLEDGE**   3
- Before the beginning   4
- What is reality?   5
- Nothing we can prove   6
- But have we outgrown our need for God?   7
- Believing impossible things?   8
- Who? Why?   10
- What is truth?   11
- No worshipper is safe   12
- A thought in the mind of the Lord   13

2   **GOD WITH US?**   15
- Why should God be hidden?   16
- 'According to the Scriptures'   18
- Hear the Word of the Lord   19
- The God who never was   20
- The God who is   21
- Signs and wonders   22
- Beyond our reach   23
- Taking the centre to the margins   24
- The Alpha and the Omega   25
- God is...   26

3   **A SUBVERSIVE GOSPEL**   29
- An Intelligence Officer reports   30
- The Gospel is subversive   32
- Upsetting – but exhilarating   33
- Family ties are questioned   34
- Shock waves hit the church   35
- A faith for outsiders   36
- Let the dead bury the dead   37
- Learn from a crook?   38
- Good to defeat evil   39
- Something to communicate?   40

4	**FIGHTINGS AND FEARS**	**41**
	Have you ever been lost?	42
	The knowledge of good and evil	43
	Wrestling in the dark	44
	'Do not let your hearts be troubled'	45
	If only...	46
	I've had enough, Lord'	48
	Not there when needed?	50
	Utterly forsaken?	52
	Defeat or victory?	54
5	**RESURRECTION!**	**57**
	The Roman Governor gives a press conference	58
	The reality of the cross	60
	An outrageous claim – unless...	61
	On the edge of the unknown	62
	A shatteringly new perspective	63
	'I believe in the resurrection of the body and the life everlasting'	64
	Resurrection now!	65
	A living Lord!	66
	At the Communion Table	67
	So what is Plan B?	68
6	**TRANSFORMATION SCENE**	**69**
	How long, O Lord, how long?	70
	Beginning at Pentecost	73
	Fruit of the Spirit	74
	A spiritual awakening	75
	A matter of doing the right thing	76
	Private enterprise transformed	77
	A mission to heal	78
	Be an angel!	80
	Not only an angel – be a saint!	81
	Cry to the winds	82
7	**PEOPLE OF GOD ?**	**83**
	An answer to prayer	84
	A true high churchmanship	87
	Part of the Body of Christ	88
	Born again Christians	90

	Not a religion, but a way	91
	The church where we worship	92
	The stories that count	94
	One church, one faith, one Lord	95
	Two prayers for the people of God	96

8	**THE TRIVIAL ROUND**	**97**
	The eternal Adam	98
	Starting at home	101
	Neighbours!	102
	A proper pride	103
	Part of the action	104
	The years pass and the world changes	105
	Heaven in my heart, but my feet on the ground	106
	Weakness and strength	107
	Technology – old and new	108

9	**WIDER HORIZONS**	**109**
	Early retirement?	110
	Rights – and responsibilities	111
	The basic stuff of life	112
	A call to share the earth's bounty	114
	'Be biased towards the poor'	115
	Not 'Why did it happen?' but, 'How can I help?'	116
	A vision of peaceful co-existence	117
	God of all peoples?	118
	Living, we must learn to live	119

10	**THE END IS THE BEGINNING**	**121**
	The inescapable fact of death	122
	Whence comes the dream?	124
	The four horsemen of the Apocalypse	125
	But if not... !	126
	Is heaven really out there?	128
	Plenty of accommodation !	129
	Judgement	130
	The reality of Hell	131
	The Saviour	132
	A light beyond the darkness	133

Acknowledgments   **135**

Introduction

Yes –
I believe!
Yet, what exactly is it that I believe?

My faith refuses to be parcelled
into a neat and tidy system;
it is not a well lit panorama,
but rather,
areas of brightness
leaving much in shadow;
and it asks awkward questions of me,
not least those questions
which make me
face up to my failures as a Christian.

And so what follows
is not a systematic statement,
not a creed;
nor is it a confident assertion,
'Thus says the Lord';
but rather,
through a paragraph here,
a verse there,
snatches of dialogue,
fables,
prayers –
I have taken my faith
and turned it inside out
and upside down,
that at the end
I may the more surely say –

I believe!

Chapter 1
Beyond all Knowledge

I do not know what I may appear to the world, but to myself I seem to have been only a boy playing on the sea-shore, and diverting myself in now and then finding a smoother pebble or a prettier shell than ordinary, whilst the great ocean of truth lay all undiscovered before me.
Isaac Newton. Brewster's Memoirs of Newton

My own suspicion is that the universe is not only queerer than we suppose but queerer than we can suppose.
J B S Haldane (1892-1964) quoted in Kenneth Clark's 'Civilisation'

For now we see in a mirror, dimly, but then we will see face to face. Now I know only in part; then I will know fully, even as I have been fully known.
St Paul. 1 Corinthians 13,12 NRSV

- **Before the beginning**
- **What is reality?**
- **Nothing we can prove**
- **But have we outgrown our need for God?**
- **Believing impossible things?**
- **Who? Why?**
- **What is truth?**
- **No worshipper is safe**
- **A thought in the mind of the Lord**

Beyond all knowledge

Before the beginning

In the beginning when God created the heavens and the earth, the earth was a formless void. (Genesis 1:1 NRSV)

Before the beginning there was nothing,
nothing;
there wasn't any earth,
there wasn't any sea,
there wasn't any sky;
there was nothing that could run,
nothing that could swim,
nothing that could fly;
nothing that could speak,
nothing that could laugh,
nothing that could cry;
nothing;
nothing;
not even a single creepy crawly.

Then all of a sudden there was something,
something –
a thought in the mind of God.
And out of that thought came space
and stars, and suns,
and planets and moons
and light and dark
and cold and heat
and SOUND...

> And the stars sang out to the glory of their Maker,
> sang as they moved at a gathering pace,
> sang as they twinkled in the new made heavens,
> sang as they danced through the clear clean space –
> > 'Praise to the thought that dreamed us,
> > praise to the skill that made us,
> > praise to the God who orders all
> > and evermore sustains us.'

From 'The Maker of Things', a light hearted cantata about our place in creation.

What Is reality?

In the beginning was the Word, and the Word was with God, and the Word was God... All things came into being through him.
(John 1:1 & 3 NRSV)

Not just one,
but a universe of universes;
starting from nothing,
or next to nothing,
in a big,
a very,
very,
very,
big bang...

And nothing is solid?
Everything is energy in tension?
If all is as insubstantial
as modern science suggests,
maybe it is not so foolish to believe
that the whole of creation
is nothing more
and nothing less
than the expression of the thoughts of God.

> *We are so enthralled*
> *by the revelations of science*
> *and the products of technology*
> *that we often forget, Lord,*
> *just how insubstantial they really are.*
> *Help us to come to a proper sense*
> *of values and priorities,*
> *and stimulate us to reach out*
> *to eternal realities*
> *and the enduring kingdom*
> *of which,*
> *in this world,*
> *we only get tantalising glimpses.*

Nothing we can prove

It is by faith that we understand that the universe was created by God's word. (Hebrews 11:3 GNB)

There is no scientific way
by which we can prove that God exists.
We may track down minute particles,
bursts of energy, or whatever may be
the ultimate building blocks of the universe;
we may weigh, measure, analyse, assess
any and every part of creation –
but we cannot analyse the Creator.

Where science cannot reach
we live by faith,
faith in the God whose nature
has been revealed in Jesus Christ;
a God who is ready to become utterly vulnerable
and calls on us to share this vulnerability.

And we are called to stake our all
on this universe being God's universe
and the way of Christ –
> the way of the Saviour
> who welcomes the outcast,
> and washes his disciples feet –
being the way of life for us,
however much we may stumble
as we try to walk in it.

> *Lord, strengthen my faith
> and stiffen my resolve,
> so that however much
> I make a mess of things,
> I may continue to try to walk
> in the way of Christ
> all the days of my life.*

But have we outgrown our need for God?

Some scoffed; others said, 'We will hear you on this subject some other time'. (Acts 17:32 REB)

In this fragile, ever changing world,
yesterday's certainties
have been superseded
by today's discoveries,
and today's discoveries will soon be outdated
by tomorrow's revelations.
New facts about the nature of the universe
are constantly coming to light;
the technological revolution continues...

Has the human race then,
outgrown it's need for God?
Are we more humane?
More honest?
Less self seeking?
More compassionate?

We acclaim the benefits which flow from
an ever developing technology,
yet fear the potential for evil
which that new knowledge has unleashed.

> *Help me, Lord, to truly value*
> *human wisdom and human achievement*
> *and to give praise generously*
> *where praise is due;*
> *but save me from being seduced*
> *by human knowledge and skills*
> *into forgetting that you,*
> *who are the source of*
> *all our knowledge, all our skills,*
> *can alone give meaning*
> *and direction to our living.*

Believing impossible things?

'I can't believe that!' said Alice.
'Can't you?' the Queen said in pitying tone.
'Try again: draw a long breath and shut your eyes.'
Alice laughed. 'There's no use trying,' she said:
'one can't believe impossible things.'
'I daresay you haven't had much practice,' said the Queen.
'When I was your age, I always did it for half an hour a day. Why sometimes I've believed as many as six impossible things before breakfast.'
(Lewis Carroll 'Alice Through The Looking Glass')

We walk by faith, not by sight. (2 Corinthians 5:7 NRSV)

Having faith
is not a matter of believing impossible things
but of trusting where we have good reason to trust.
We act in faith
each time we have a meal,
each time we send a letter,
each time we go on a journey;
indeed there is little in life
which does not depend upon an act of faith
based on and justified by experience.

To their contemporaries,
what poor misguided fools
those first century Christians looked.
How out of date we look
to many of our own acquaintances.
What does it matter?
We take the leap of faith,
and commit ourselves joyfully to the Lord of life.

Beyond all knowledge

In a society marked by affluent pessimism
we proclaim the age of the resurrection.
In the face of sorrows, fears and downright wickedness
we proclaim a message of hope, renewal and forgiveness.

We proclaim that the Lord
who was rejected and crucified is risen,
and reaching out in love to all who will receive him.

This we believe!
And this is our message for the world!

> *O Lord let thy mercy lighten upon us*
> *as our trust is in thee.*
> *O Lord in Thee have I trusted,*
> *Let me never be confounded*

(Te Deum BCP)

Who? Why?

Moses replied, "When I go to the Israelites and say to them, 'The God of your ancestors sent me to you,' they will ask me, 'What is his name?' So what can I tell them?" God said, "I AM WHO I AM".
(Exodus 3:13-14 GNB)

Who are you?
What is your name, your nature,
what reality lies behind that little word, "GOD"?

Like Moses I too have questions.
Why in a world of breathtaking beauty
and intricate design,
are there earthquakes, volcanic eruptions,
dramatic climate changes?
Why do we have to face
such awful diseases,
such widespread suffering,
so much downright evil?

And so I could continue
asking why? why? why?

But I also am confronted with
'I AM WHO I AM –
I WILL BE WHAT I WILL BE.'
and I realise that I cannot hope to probe beyond
the 'otherness' of God;
that there are some questions
to which, in this world,
I will never find the answer.

> God before all, God in all,
> I believe you mean me to use to the full
> the mind you have given me,
> that you mean me to ask probing questions;
> but help me also to recognise my limitations
> and to trust you for what I cannot understand.

What is truth?

You will know the truth, and the truth will make you free.
(John 8:32 NRSV)

I am the way, the truth, and the life. (John 14:6 NRSV)

Everyone who belongs to the truth listens to my voice.
Pilate asked him, 'What is truth?' (John 18:37,38 NRSV)

Stories provide answers
to life's most insistent questions.
Both ancient myths
and modern theories
offer explanations
which may be confirmed, developed, or replaced
in the light of further experience.

We are at best seekers
whose understanding of truth is partial.
Both myths and theories,
religion and science,
must face continual challenge
as we become aware of fresh aspects
of God's eternal, unchanging truths.

And the most important quest for Christians
must surely be,
through confrontation with the Gospel,
to learn ever more of the truth about themselves
and the way in which life is meant to be lived.

> *Lord, we pray that you will so deal with us*
> *that we may learn ever more about ourselves*
> *and the transforming power of your love for us.*
> *Strengthen our resolve to know and to live*
> *by the truth you have revealed through a human life,*
> *and in your mercy bring us back to the way when we stray.*

Beyond all knowledge

No worshipper is safe

Give unto the Lord the glory due unto his name; worship the Lord in the beauty of holiness. (Psalm 29:2 AV)

No worshipper is safe.
In worship we stand on the edge of mystery,
we come in awe and wonder,
not certainty.
We worship, praying
that we may be ready to take
the one step which can be taken,
to do the one thing that cries out to be done,
however unthinkable or illogical it may be.
We come seeking to be open to the God
who is ever creating,
ever renewing.

Worship can be disturbing,
even dangerous.
For Abraham, responding to God
led to a pilgrimage into the unknown. [1]
Moses was told to return to Egypt
from which he had fled in fear for his life. [2]
Elijah, waiting in a cave at Horeb for a little comfort,
was directed back to the struggle
from which he had sought to escape. [3]
Worship can be the launch pad for renewal
but also, at times,
for revolution!

> *Lord, teach me how to worship, patiently,*
> *but expectantly,*
> *how to wait, how to listen,*
> *that I may be ready to recognise and respond*
> *to whatever you would say to me,*
> *however disconcerting it may be.*

(1) Genesis 12.1ff
(2) Exodus 3.1ff
(3) 1 Kings 19.13ff

A thought in the mind of the Lord

and God said, 'Let there be...' (Genesis 1 NRSV)

And the Lord God listened,
and the Lord God looked,
and then the Lord God said –

You have worshipped trees,
you have worshipped rocks,
you have worshipped the sun
and the moon and the sea,
you have worshipped the things
you have made with your hands
and forgotten that all of them come from me.

For there's nothing that is,
and there's nothing that was
and there's nothing that yet
is to come to be,
that hasn't begun as a thought in my mind
for there's nothing exists
but it comes from me.

And everything made
that ever there was,
is given to you without payment or fee
but the things that you grasp
you will only enjoy
if you treat them with care
and give glory to me.

Remember that everything, everything about you,
things that you waste and things that you hoard;
remember that everything, everything about you,
began as a thought in the mind of the Lord.

From 'The Maker of Things', a light hearted cantata about our place in creation.

Beyond all knowledge

Chapter 2

God With Us?

As I went through the city and looked carefully at the objects of your worship, I found among them an altar with the inscription, 'To an unknown god.' What therefore you worship as unknown, this I proclaim to you. (Acts 17:23 NRSV)

Then Job answered: 'Today also my complaint is bitter; his hand is heavy despite my groaning. Oh, that I knew where I might find him, that I might come even to his dwelling! (Job 23:1-3 NRSV)

- **Why should God be hidden?**
- **'According to the Scriptures'**
- **Hear the Word of the Lord**
- **The God who never was**
- **The God who is**
- **Signs and wonders**
- **Beyond our reach**
- **Taking the centre to the margins**
- **The Alpha and the Omega**
- **God is...**

Why should God be hidden?

'Lord show us the Father; we ask no more'. (John 14:8 REB)

'I saw the Lord'. (Isaiah 6:1 REB)

Why should God be hidden?
Why not a world wide
multi-media broadcast?

The BBC could give the lead –
'The Lord God Almighty will speak tonight'.
They'd start with interviews of course;
statesmen, TV personalities, world church leaders,
and, to give proper balance,
humanists, atheists,
the sports personality of the year
and the person in the street suddenly confronted by a microphone.

Then, as the moment approached,
appropriate music – Handel, Bach, Palestrina –
nothing too modern;
afterwards, massed choirs singing 'How great thou art',
reports from correspondents world wide
and votes from the studio audience…

But God cannot be revealed
except to those tuned
to receive a very different type of transmission;
women and men who long with all their hearts
to glimpse eternal realities.

Isaiah 'saw the Lord'
only after the bottom had fallen out of his world.
He went into the Temple in near despair
and came out aware that the whole world
was already full of the glory of God.

In the year that King Uzziah died, I saw the Lord sitting on a throne, high and lofty; and the hem of his robe filled the Temple. Seraphs were in attendance above him; each had six wings: with two they covered their faces, and with two they covered their feet, and with two they flew. And one called to another and said:
          "Holy, holy, holy is the Lord of hosts;
          the whole earth is full of his glory."
The pivots on the thresholds shook at the voices of those who called, and the house was filled with smoke. And I said: Woe is me! I am lost, for I am a man of unclean lips, and I live among a people of unclean lips; yet mine eyes have seen the King, the Lord of hosts!"

(Isaiah 6:1-5 NRSV)

'According to the Scriptures'

Your word is a lamp to my feet and a light to my path.
(Psalm 119:105 NRSV)

But we have this treasure in clay jars. (2 Corinthians 4:7 NRSV)

And the Word became flesh and lived among us, and we have seen his glory, the glory as of a father's only son, full of grace and truth.
(John 1:14 NRSV)

He charged us before God and his blessed angels, to follow him no farther than he followed Christ. And if God should reveal anything to us by any other instrument of his, to be as ready to receive it, as ever we were to receive any truth by his ministry; for he was very confident the Lord had more truth and light yet to break forth out of His holy Word. *(John Robinson's farewell to the Pilgrim Fathers)*

The Holy Scriptures;
God's self revelation
through a strand of human history;
the very Word of God to direct our living!
Yes,
but a Word transmitted
through fallible human beings.

A fresh Word is spoken:
but now it is self revelation through a human life.
The Word becomes flesh!
And it is in the light of this living Word,
to which the Scriptures bear witness,
that the Scriptures as a whole
must be understood
and interpreted.

We thank you, Lord, for all who compiled, copied, translated or in any other way shared in passing on to us the Holy Scriptures. Teach us to use wisely this great gift, that through the Scriptures we may be drawn ever closer to you.

Hear the Word of the Lord

Hear the word of the Lord. (Isaiah 1:10 NRSV and many other places)

My word...shall not return to me empty, but it shall accomplish that which I purpose.

(Isaiah 55:11 NRSV)

Hearing the 'Word of the Lord',
really hearing,
can be a shattering experience
transforming all our priorities
and making many of the things
about which we have been praying
appear petty and irrelevant.

The Bible bears witness to God speaking
and women and men either responding
or refusing to listen.
This same God
surely has a Word for us,
speaking to our own time
and our own condition,
if only we will hear it.

To be solely concerned with the response
God will make to our prayers
is to stand Bible priorities on their head.
What really matters
is the response we make
to the Word
which the living God addresses
directly to us.

> *Lord, teach me how to listen*
> *for your Word speaking in my heart,*
> *and strengthen my will to respond,*
> *to that word, whatever it may require of me.*

The God who never was

Whoever has seen me has seen the Father. How can you say, 'Show us the Father?' Do you not believe that I am in the Father and the Father is in me? (John 14:9-10 NRSV)

If God was in Christ
then God has always been –
will always be –
as Christ was,
for God is surely all of a piece.
If God is love, God has never been other than love.

The God who told his chosen people
to slay or cast out all who stood in their way
never was,
however much some
may have convinced themselves
that this was what was required of them.

The God of bloody crusades and religious wars
and all other ills that flow from fanatical extremism
never was,
however much men or women
may persuade themselves
that these things are the will of God.

The coming of Jesus sets the record straight.
To see Jesus, the Christ,
is to see the Eternal Father
reaching out with nail torn hands
willing, longing,
in love to embrace us all.

> *God of love, teach us what it really means*
> *to love you and, for your sake,*
> *to love all your children*
> *with heart, soul, mind and strength*

The God who is

For Jews demand signs and Greeks desire wisdom, but we proclaim Christ crucified, a stumbling block to Jews and foolishness to Gentiles, but to those who are called, both Jews and Greeks, Christ the power of God and the wisdom of God. (1 Corinthians 1:22-24 NRSV)

Following Jesus,
we find ourselves in that strange domain
where the Prince of Peace says enigmatically,
'I come not to bring peace but a sword'.
Where the King of Kings and Lord of Lords
is a poor man with no regular home of his own
who is ultimately rejected and crucified.

We find ourselves serving a Lord
who is particularly understanding of sins
over which we get greatly concerned,
and passionately scathing about sins
we seek to make respectable.

There was nothing bland or sterilised
about Jesus of Nazareth.
He didn't mind his disciples eating with dirty hands. [1]
He didn't mind grasping a leper. [2]
He was quite ready to sit down
and have a serious conversation with a prostitute. [3]
On the other hand,
when it came to those who thought they knew it all,
he certainly didn't mince his words if need arose.

> *Do not allow us to evade the truth, Lord,*
> *that we ourselves still have much to learn*
> *about the ways of God.*
> *So deal with us, we pray,*
> *that we may become more fit*
> *to be called part of your body,*
> *more able to serve you in the world.*

(1) Mark 7.1ff
(2) Mark 1.40ff
(3) John 4.7ff

Signs and wonders

This will be a sign for you. (Luke 2:12 NRSV)

Is not this the carpenter, the son of Mary, and brother of James and Joses and Judas and Simon, and are not his sisters here with us?
(Mark 6:3 NRSV)

Was this really a sign from God,
a baby born to an insignificant couple
in the stable of an overcrowded inn?
True a few shepherds came
with a story of angel messengers;
but who else in Bethlehem showed any interest?
Was that really the best the Almighty could do?

We still find it difficult to accept
that God is to be found in the ordinary
rather than the extraordinary;
yet our Lord lived a human life,
learned the trade of a carpenter,
experienced failure as well as success,
and, like us, had to wrestle with temptation.

He was truly human, yet fully in touch with God;
and through his living
we learn that acts of God
are part of our very existence.
We may fail to recognise them,
but we cannot possibly exclude them.

*Teach me, Lord,
how to seek the signs of your presence,
not so much in breathtaking wonders,
as in the everyday events
that make up most of my living.*

/ Beyond our reach

They looked toward the wilderness, and the glory of the Lord appeared in the cloud. (Exodus 16:10 NRSV)

As they were watching, he was lifted up, and a cloud took him out of their sight. (Acts 1:9 NRSV)

That the glory of God should be
enveloped in impenetrable cloud
is a direct challenge to an age
that would have all secrets laid bare,
every thought of any public figure anticipated,
and the highlights of every major speech reported
before it is even delivered.

There is no way in which this process
can be applied to the Almighty.
All our accumulated wisdom,
all our technological developments,
all our formidable research facilities,
can only bring us to the edge of the cloud
to wonder and to worship.

But Jesus, who lived, died, and rose again,
has entered into that cloud,
taking all that it means to be human
into the very being of God.
Thus the God who is beyond our knowing
knows us intimately,
reaches out to us lovingly
and accepts us as we actually are.

> *Almighty God,*
> *we praise you that through our Lord Jesus Christ*
> *you knowingly and lovingly accept us*
> *despite all our follies.*
> *Help us, we pray, to become more worthy of that love*
> *and to reflect more of it to others in our daily living.*

Taking the centre to the margins

I have not come to call respectable people, but outcasts.
(Mark 2:17 GNB)

Come to me, all of you who are tired from carrying heavy loads.
(Matthew 11:28 GNB)

God, who is at the centre of all things,
through Christ took the centre to the margins.
And so it is that –
when we are most aware of our failures,
most ashamed of our follies,
fragile,
off balance;
when our world appears to be
disintegrating around us
and our self confidence has vanished;
then, above all times,
we may be sure that God is at hand.

And we may trust the God
who is at the centre of all things
to deal with us just as our Lord in his earthly ministry
dealt with those he found on the margins –
personally,
intimately,
and out of the immensity of his love.

>Painful as it may be,
>I need your help, Lord,
>to make me recognise and acknowledge
>my most besetting sins,
>my deepest needs for healing,
>that I may be able to receive the forgiveness
>and the restoration which you alone can give.

The Alpha and the Omega

'I am the Alpha and the Omega,' says the Lord God, who is and who was and who is to come, the Almighty.
(Revelation 1:8 NRSV)

We know that all things work together for good for those who love God.
(Romans 8:28 NRSV)

Why did it all begin –
the world,
the universe,
everything that is,
life itself?
And where is it going,
towards what end is it moving?

The Bible writers
addressed these age old,
yet contemporary questions
using various images
coloured by the times in which they lived;
but none doubted
that just as the beginning was with God
so too will be the climax.

Whatever clouds may darken our skies
we are in the hands of the Almighty
whose purposes are good;
and we may trust
that like the beginning,
the end will be with God.

> *Lord, may we ever live in the faith*
> *that we, with all things,*
> *are in your strong hands*
> *and that nothing can prevent*
> *the ultimate fulfilment*
> *of your loving purposes.*

God Is...

God is the Word
which became flesh and dwelt among us. *(John 1:14)*

God is the Light
which no darkness can totally obliterate. *(John 1:5)*

God is the Peace
which reaches out to us in life's fiercest storms. *(John 14:27)*

God is the Hope
which gives confidence of a brighter future. *(Romans 15:13)*

God is the Comfort
which reaches even our deepest sorrows. *(2 Corinthians 1:3)*

God is the Healing
for self inflicted wounds of wilfulness and sin. *(Revelation 22:2)*

God is the Forgiveness
which shoulders the burden of our follies. *(1 John 1:9)*

God is the Love
which never writes us off, whatever we have done. *(John 3:16)*

God is the Life
which holds us secure to the gates of death and beyond. *(John 11:25)*

> *For God so loved the world that he gave his only Son, so that everyone who believes in him may not perish but may have eternal life. Indeed, God did not send the Son into the world to condemn the world, but in order that the world might be saved through him.*
>
> *(John 3:16-17 NRSV)*

*God, all in all, may I wake each morning
to look on the world with awe and wonder,
not asking whether you are at work,
but rather asking how I may better recognise
the signs of your presence round about me
and how I may best serve you in the day ahead.*

Chapter 3

A Subversive Gospel

And the crowd came together again, so that they could not even eat. When his family heard it. they went out to restrain him, for people were saying, 'He has gone out of his mind'.
(Mark 3:20-21 NRSV)

He was teaching and saying, "is it not written, 'My house shall be called a house of prayer for all nations'? But you have made it a den of robbers." And when the chief priests heard it, they kept looking for a way to kill him; for they were afraid of him.
(Mark 11.17,18 NRSV)

- **An Intelligence Officer reports**
- **The Gospel is subversive**
- **Upsetting – but exhilarating**
- **Family ties are questioned**
- **Shock waves hit the church**
- **A faith for outsiders**
- **Let the dead bury the dead**
- **Learn from a crook?**
- **Good to defeat evil**
- **Something to communicate?**

An Intelligence Officer reports

Commander	What have you learnt?
Officer	His present base is Capernaum, Sir, though he comes from Nazareth. Unmarried. Eldest son. Worked with his father, and took over as village carpenter when the old man died.
Commander	Any history?
Officer	None Sir. He was well thought of, good workman they say, no excesses, no politics.
Commander	So, what happened?
Officer	A few months ago he handed everything over to a brother and came down here to visit that wild prophet who was baptising by the Jordan crossing.
Commander	Plenty of people did that. Even some of the troops went down and got a flea in their ear.
Officer	The difference here Sir, is that I've discovered that they were related. Cousins. Our man disappears after visiting the baptiser, and then reappears after Herod executed him.
Commander	Well that's a relief. If he is just carrying on where the other left off we haven't much to worry about.
Officer	I don't think it's quite as simple as that, Sir.
Commander	Why so, is he preaching revolution?

Officer	No, not revolution, but what he says is still unsettling.
Commander	For example?
Officer	Take the policy of conscripting men for labouring jobs...
Commander	Don't worry about that. All the hot heads tell them they should resist, it doesn't make the slightest bit of difference.
Officer	But that's the point, Sir, he doesn't tell them to resist. He says, 'If you're compelled to go one mile volunteer to go another'.
Commander	You're joking.
Officer	No Sir.
Commander	Then he is.
Officer	No Sir, he means it, and he tells them to accept injury without hitting back and to forgive enemies any wrong they've done them.
Commander	And they accept it?
Officer	Crowds grow bigger all the time.
Commander	I see what you mean. What's he up to I wonder? And say the troops began to listen to him. Where would we be then? D'you know, I begin to think you are right. This man could be dangerous.

The Gospel Is subversive

There's no two ways about it –
the Gospel is subversive!
When Jesus was crucified,
the charges were –
blasphemy, subverting the faith,
and treason, subverting the state.

Paul, preaching Christ, declared
*'God has chosen things without rank or standing,
mere nothings, to overthrow the existing order.'* [1]
Luke has Mary singing –
*'He hath put down the mighty from their seat:
and hath exalted the humble and meek.
He hath filled the hungry with good things
and the rich he hath sent empty away.'* [2]
You can't get much more subversive than that!

Even the Beatitudes are highly subversive; [3]
why, if the idea once caught on that happiness
had nothing to do with possessions
there'd be mass unemployment
and our whole economy would grind to a halt.

Don't look to Christ for a quiet life,
he's a revolutionary,
always has been, always will be;
stay with him,
and he'll turn your life upside down.

> *Lord Jesus Christ,
> never let me become so set in my ways
> that I become immune to the challenge of the Gospel;
> save me, I pray, from ever imagining
> that I have no more to learn from you.*

(1) 1 Corinthians 1:28 REB
(2) Luke 1:52,53 BCP
(3) Matthew 5:3ff. Luke 6:20ff

Upsetting - but exhilarating

No one can see the kingdom of God unless he is born again. (John 3:2 GNB)

Whoever does not receive the Kingdom of God like a child will never enter it. (Mark 10:15 GNB)

To an astonished Nicodemus
Jesus said, 'You must be born again,'
and he told equally startled disciples
that to enter the kingdom
they needed to become like little children.

It is not easy for us to acknowledge
the need to be born again
and not just once,
but many times in the course of our lives.
It is not a comfortable thought that the Gospel
is likely to go on challenging our values
and our way of looking at things
for as long as we live.
Yet If we really expose ourselves to the Gospel
we must always be ready
for unexpected, unwanted ideas to break in;
ready for a new unsettling light to be thrown
on what we thought long since settled.
Uncomfortable it may be,
but thank God for the Gospel,
for it is also exhilarating and life giving –
There is nothing to replace it.

> *However old I may grow, Lord,*
> *I pray that you will keep a youthful spirit within me,*
> *ready for whatever new adventure*
> *you may call me to undertake,*
> *until at last, the time comes for me*
> *to enter upon the greatest adventure of all.*

Family ties are questioned

'Your mother and your brothers and sisters are outside, asking for you'. ... And looking at those who sat round him, he said, 'Here are my mother and my brothers! Whoever does the will of God is my brother and sister and mother." (Mark 3:33-35 NRSV)

It wasn't a social call.
His relatives had turned out in force
to put pressure on him to end this dangerous ministry
which they feared threatened them all.
Jesus should return to the carpenter's shop
and his place at the head of the family.
Family ties were strong.
He would have felt the pain of refusing to go with them;
but the call of God had to come first.

'Do not think that I have come to bring peace to the earth; I have not come to bring peace, but a sword. For I have come to set a man against his father, and a daughter against her mother, and a daughter-in-law against her mother-in-law; and one's foes will be members of one's own household.' (Matthew 10:34-36 NRSV)

It doesn't have to be that way of course;
but there will always be some
who will only be able to follow the call they have heard
in the face of disapproval,
failure to understand
and maybe, downright hostility,
on the part of those
to whom they owe much
and for whom they have the deepest affection.

> *We pray for those who face such a difficult choice;*
> *for family members who are bitter*
> *through their failure to recognise*
> *the divine imperative;*
> *and for the ultimate healing*
> *of such broken relationships.*

Shock waves hit the church

Come you that are blessed... For I was hungry and you gave me food. I was thirsty and you gave me something to drink, I was a stranger and you welcomed me, I was naked and you gave me clothing, I was sick and you took care of me, I was in prison and you visited me.
(Matthew 25:34-36 NRSV)

They settled down anticipating
the familiar story of the last judgement,
the one where the favoured sheep
were separated from the unwanted goats;
they always found it comforting,
for wasn't the Lord their shepherd,
and they his faithful sheep?

But it wasn't the familiar story!
Jesus set up shock waves
by declaring that there were surprises ahead,
they might not be among the sheep after all!

If he was to be believed
what mattered in the sight of God
was not their impeccable law abiding behaviour;
not even their faithful support of the church;
but the practical help they had given
or failed to give,
to the desperately poor,
the disadvantaged,
the outcasts and the misfits –
Why, if you believed that,
the sheep might include
people who never went to church at all!

> *Teach us, Lord,*
> *to be generous in word and deed,*
> *to recognise you even in the most unlikely people*
> *and to reach out to those who need our help*
> *willingly and lovingly, for your sake.*

A Subversive Gospel

A faith for outsiders

It wasn't so much what he said,
though he did speak of
the lost coin, the lost sheep, the lost son
and of widespread rejoicing
when they were found.[1]

No, It was in the way he lived
that Jesus revealed how God
bends over backwards for the outsider.
> He grasped the leper.[2]
> He restored dignity to the woman
> dragged to his feet
> by a vicious, self righteous mob.[3]
> He picked the unpopular Zaachaeus
> out of the crowds
> and invited himself to his home
> without uttering a single word
> about repenting and being converted.[4]

Godly people found this shocking;
but the Christ who was crucified outside the city limits
and who In his dying agony
promised a criminal crucified beside him
a place in paradise;[5]
that Christ still reaches out in love to the outsider,
and so, reaches out to us all.

> *Thanks be to God for a love so great*
> *that it reaches out*
> *to each and every human soul,*
> *ready to take us as we are,*
> *and lead us gently into*
> *the ways of the kingdom.*

(1) Luke 15
(2) Mark 1:40,41
(3) John 8:1ff
(4) Luke 19:1ff
(5) Luke 23:42,43

Let the dead bury the dead

Let the dead bury their own dead; but as for you, go and proclaim the kingdom of God. (Luke 9:60 NRSV)

The voice comes ringing down the ages.
'You are not called
to bolster up the existing order,
but to submit the existing order
to the searching judgments of God.
There are more than enough people
enmeshed in customs and tradition,
leave them, the dead, to bury the dead;
your work is to go and proclaim
the kingdom of God'.

It is a call to live,
not so much 'good' lives as prophetic lives.
So often we think of the church
as the community
in which we must make every effort
to avoid striking a discordant note;
yet Jesus Christ was a rebel,
shocking not only the Pharisees
but his own disciples,
shaking them, frightening them,
forcing them to think and to grow...

'Leave the dead to bury the dead,' he said,
'your business is to proclaim the kingdom
of the ever living, ever renewing God.'

> *Lord, help us to look forward, not back,*
> *show us how to relate the Gospel to our present age*
> *and enable us to be true heralds of your kingdom.*

Learn from a crook?

And his master commended the dishonest manager because he had acted shrewdly ...

It's outrageous!
How could you possibly take this story
about a thoroughly dishonest steward
being praised by the master he's cheated
and use it in church?

Or did Jesus,
with a twinkle in his eye,
deliberately tell it in the hope
that it would make people in the churches,
people like me,
sit up and take notice?

The man has been found out,
he is losing his job
and, unless he does something quickly,
there is a bleak future ahead of him.

Was Jesus saying
that, rogue that he was,
this man recognised a crisis
and –
instead of just moaning about it,
or leisurely taking steps
to set up a committee to consider and report –
with a sense of urgency
often lacking amongst the respectable and the good,
he got on and did something about it?

... for the children of this age are more shrewd in dealing with their own generation than are the children of light. (Luke 16:8 NRSV)

A Subversive Gospel

Good to defeat evil

Do not let evil defeat you; instead, conquer evil with good.
(Romans 12:21 GNB)

Why do we tell children to 'be good',
when what we really mean is
that we want them to find something to do
which wont disturb us?
How easily they can grow up with the idea
that goodness is simply a matter
of being quiet and inoffensive.

Yet when he discovered that one of his flock was missing
the good shepherd didn't sit down
and eat his bread, cheese and pickled onion
with a look of pious resignation;
he went out into the rough country
and searched for the lost until he'd found it.[1]

Our Lord broke most of the rules for being good
and the 'good' people were scandalised.
'Look at him', they said, 'look at the company he keeps,
why he doesn't even observe the Sabbath as he should'.[2]
With Christ it was a matter of reaching out
in total self giving to where the need was greatest.
This is the offensive
which shifts the balance in the world,
This is the true goodness which ultimately defeats evil.

> *God, source of all that is good,*
> *do not allow us to ignore the difference*
> *between 'being good'*
> *and doing right by the needy,*
> *the defenceless, the wronged.*
> *Give us, we pray, the will and the stamina*
> *to pursue that true goodness*
> *which alone can defeat evil.*

(1) Matthew 18:12 & John 10:11
(2) Mark 2:15 & 2:23

Credo

Something to communicate?

A message for the world, you say?
You've certainly come to the right place,
we have all the expertise you'll ever need.
Welcome to 'Weasel Words',
communicators supreme to Planet Earth.

Do you fancy an aggressive, thrusting, campaign,
the hard sell?
None can do it better.
Or maybe you'd prefer the subtle innuendo
feeding ideas subconsciously into people's minds?
We call that the 'virus technique'
and have made it our speciality.

No?

Other models?
The seed growing silently,
the leaven in the dough?
I can't say I've met them,
they sound singularly ineffective,
not our style at all.

Well, try it your way if you must,
When you realise you're not getting anywhere
you know where to find us –
Weasel Words, Inferno Lane;
we'll be expecting you.

> *Despite our weaknesses*
> *we must strive to proclaim the Gospel*
> *by living the Gospel.*
> *In caring for others for Christ's sake*
> *we must discover our real selves;*
> *for the more truly we become Christ's witnesses*
> *the more surely we shall ourselves be changed.*

Chapter 4

Fighting and Fears

*Just as I am, though tossed about
with many a conflict, many a doubt,
fightings and fears within, without,
O Lamb of God, I come.*

(Charlotte Elliott)

*No, when the fight begins within himself,
a man's worth something. God stoops o'er his head,
Satan looks up between his feet – both tug –
he's left, himself, in the middle: the soul wakes
and grows. Prolong that battle through his life!
Never leave growing till the life to come!*

(Robert Browning. Bishop Blougram's Apology)

- **Have you ever been lost?**
- **The knowledge of good and evil**
- **Wrestling in the dark**
- **'Do not let your heart be troubled'**
- **If only...**
- **'I've had enough, Lord'**
- **Not there when needed?**
- **Utterly forsaken?**
- **Defeat or victory?**

Fighting and Fears

Have you ever been lost?

Have you ever been lost,
so utterly lost
that there's nowhere on earth you can go;
when you find you're adrift
on a sea of despair,
nothing above or below?
> Nowhere on earth you can go,
> nothing above or below.

Have you stood all alone,
so completely alone,
your whole world quite fallen apart,
when you're beaten right down
with you will to live gone,
an icicle lodged in your heart?
> Nowhere on earth you can go,
> nothing above or below

Has your soul ever felt
it was stretched on a rack,
with never a moment of peace;
crippled by evil
triumphantly strong
and you're crying to death for release?
> Nowhere on earth you can go,
> nothing above or below.

And then through the darkness
comes sound of a voice
you hear, though you do not see,
'I too have been there
in the depths of despair,
but I live, will you live with me?'
> Somewhere on earth you can go
> someone above and below.

From the Musical 'One Friday'

The knowledge of good and evil

So when the woman saw that the tree was good for food, and that it was a delight to the eyes, and that the tree was to be desired to make one wise, she took of its fruit and ate; and she also gave some to her husband, who was with her, and he ate. Then the eyes of both were opened, and they knew that they were naked. (Genesis 3:6-7 NRSV)

Once the fruit of the tree of knowledge
had been eaten
in the the garden
which existed before time began,
there was no turning back.
The man and the woman
'knew that they were naked'
and sought to hide themselves from God;
but, of course,
they couldn't.

To know the difference
between good and evil;
to be capable of choice,
whilst acknowledging
how easily we get it wrong;
and being ready
to face up to guilt
and to remorse,
is part of what it means to be fully human.

> *I pray, Lord, for the will and the power*
> *to be honest with myself,*
> *and honest with you.*
> *Help me to face up to those times*
> *when I fail to do the good I recognise.*
> *Stiffen my intention to acknowledge my sin*
> *and to make every effort*
> *to put right what I know to be wrong.*

Fighting and Fears

Wrestling in the dark

*Jacob was left alone; and a man wrestled with him until daybreak...
Then he said, 'Let me go, for the day is breaking.'
But Jacob said, 'I will not let you go, unless you bless me.'*
(Genesis 32:24,26 NRSV)

Why am I suddenly assaulted
by a multitude of disquieting, nameless,
doubts and fears?
Who is the adversary
forcing me to engage
in this wrestling in the dark?
Is it demon
or angel,
destroyer
or Saviour?

Surely it must be a demon;
but do I sense God looking over it's shoulder?
Is God at hand
urging me to struggle,
urging me to grow and find blessing
through confronting my demon,
through facing up
to the battles
of the dark nights of the soul?

> *Ever present God,
> help me to wrestle with the big questions life poses,
> especially at those times when a demon whispers
> that there are no enduring values,
> that there is nothing worth striving for.
> Help me to face that demon down,
> and not to cease striving until,
> with your aid, I come through,
> having grown in the conflict
> and so found blessing.*

Do not let your heart be troubled!

Peace I leave with you; my peace I give to you. I do not give to you as the world gives. Do not let your hearts be troubled, and do not let them be afraid. (John 14:27 NRSV)

Troubled!
They were more than troubled,
they were scared out of their wits.
Even a week after the resurrection
they would still be gathering behind locked doors.
And Jesus had been troubled!
– praying in Gethsemene
that if it were possible, he might be spared
the agony which lay ahead –
And yet,
he offers us peace?

But the promise is not
that if we are good Christians
life will go smoothly,
it seldom does.
We are not offered freedom from the storms of life;
from the bitterness of failure,
from disappointments, sorrow, sickness, pain.
What we are promised is that,
come what may,
our Lord will be in it with us,
all the way.

> *We are afflicted in every way, but not crushed;*
> *perplexed, but not driven to despair;*
> *persecuted, but not forsaken;*
> *struck down, but not destroyed...*
> *because we look not at what can be seen*
> *but at what cannot be seen;*
> *for what can be seen is temporary,*
> *but what cannot be seen is eternal.*
> *(2 Corinthians 4.8,9,18.NRSV)*

Fighting and Fears

If only...

The scribes and the Pharisees brought a woman who had been caught in adultery; and making her stand before all of them, they said to him, 'Teacher, this woman was caught in the very act of committing adultery. Now in the law Moses commanded us to stone such women. Now what do you say?'...
'Let anyone among you who is without sin be the first to throw a stone at her'... 'Woman where are they? Has no one condemned you?' She said, 'No one, sir.' And Jesus said, 'Neither do I condemn you. Go your way, and from now on do not sin again.'

(John 8:3-5,7,10-11 NRSV)

Her life had been saved.
She had been given the chance
to put the past behind her and start afresh;
but, how? Where?
Dare she go back to her own community?
Whatever she did,
it certainly wouldn't be easy.

If only...

Jesus revealed a God
who reaches out lovingly
to build bridges;
to restore broken relationships;
to heal what is sick.
A God who will wipe out guilt with forgiveness.
A God who will help us to put the past behind us.

But we still have to live the rest of our lives
starting from where we are now,
there's no other way.

> Inasmuch as I've created my own problems, Lord,
> I know I have got to face up to them,
> stay with me, I pray,
> especially when the going is rough,
> and help me to make the best of whatever lies ahead.

O loving wisdom of our God!
When all was sin and shame,
a second Adam to the fight
and to the rescue came.

O wisest love! that flesh and blood,
which did in Adam fail,
should strive afresh against the foe,
should strive and should prevail.

J H Newman

'I've had enough, Lord'

'It is enough; now, O Lord, take away my life, for I am no better than my ancestors.' (1 Kings 19:4 NRSV)

Physically exhausted,
spiritually drained,
and deeply depressed,
Elijah made his way through the wilderness
to a cave where he might end his days in peace.

What did it matter that he had stood alone
against the priests of Baal;
been vindicated by fire from heaven
and the ending of the years of drought?
What did it matter
that he had run in ecstatic triumph through pouring rain,
leading the king's chariot back from Carmel to Jezreel?
Jezebel was still the power behind the throne,
nothing would really change.

Time passed.
From his shelter he witnessed
unmoved,
storms, earthquake, fire –
until in the sheer silence that followed
he discerned the presence of the Lord and heard –
'What are you doing here Elijah?
You've rested long enough,
your work is by no means yet completed,
up now, and start back upon your way!'

> Is that it, Lord?
> That we're not meant to sit back and say
> 'enough, I've done my bit'?
> Well, I'll try,
> as long as you go with me
> to renew my strength and my sense of purpose.

When the springs of my life run dry
and my spirit is heavy with grief
I must not hide in a solitary place
for my spirit must find relief;
though I've only my grief
I must share my grief
that my spirit may find relief.

When the springs of my life run dry
and my heart is racked with pain
I must not hide in a solitary place
for the springs must flow again;
though I've only my pain
I must share my pain
that the springs may flow again.

When the springs of my life run dry
and my friends are far and few
I must not hide in a solitary place
for my love must blossom anew;
through my grief and my pain
I must love once again
that my life may blossom anew.

From the play 'One Friday In Eternity'

Fighting and Fears

Not there when needed?

'Martha said to Jesus, Lord, if you had been here, my brother would not have died.'

(John 11:21 NRSV)

Where were you, Lord,
when I really needed you?
Why was there no answer to my prayers,
the most urgent prayers I have ever prayed?
Was it some fault on my part?
or was there an answer
that I didn't understand?

And it's not just me,
there are many others ...
> an unexpected diagnosis,
> a tragic accident,
> sudden redundancy,
> marriage breakup,
> an untimely death ...

Where are you, Lord,
when our little world falls apart
and we need you
so very very much?

> *Lord, when we do have to face really dark times*
> *help us to hold on to our faith*
> *that you have been that way before us*
> *and that you are with us now,*
> *sharing our distress and supporting us,*
> *even though for the moment you seem very far away.*

*If I go forward, he is not there;
or backward, I cannot perceive him;
on the left he hides, and I cannot behold him;
I turn to the right, but I cannot see him.
But he knows the way that I take...*

(Job 23:8-10 NRSV)

*For I know that my Redeemer lives,
and that at the last he will stand upon the earth;
and after my skin has been thus destroyed,
then in my flesh I shall see God.*

(Job 19:25-26 NRSV)

Fighting and Fears

Utterly forsaken?

When it was noon, darkness came over the whole land until three in the afternoon. At three o'clock Jesus cried out with a loud voice, **'My God, my God, why have you forsaken me?'**

(Mark 15:34 NRSV)

We hear this terrible cry
of one who feels
utterly alone,
cut off,
abandoned:
one from whom everything that matters in life
has been stripped away
and who is drowning
in unplumbable depths
of misery, pain
and despair.

Does this mean that In the crucified Christ
these agonies have been carried
into the very heart of God?
Can we really say
that whatever we may be called upon to face
God has been there before us,
that God knows?

> O God, is this something I can hold on to
> when everything else is falling apart;
> that you have been there before me,
> and really do know what it is to have
> no firm ground remaining
> on which to stand?
> If ever I reach such a moment of desolation
> break through, I pray,
> that I may know
> that you are indeed in the darkness with me
> and will see me through
> to the light which lies beyond.

Credo

One Friday in Eternity
a man was hung they say,
a man was hung, but why the fuss,
it happens every day;
hung, shot or crucified, who cares
it happens every day.
One Friday in Eternity
repeated every day

One Friday in Eternity
that man was God they say,
if that is true – if God was there –
it happens every day;
if God was sharing mortal pain
it happens every day.
One Friday is Eternity
repeated ever day.

From the play 'One Friday in Eternity'

Fighting and Fears

Defeat or victory?

Voice of Jesus.   **It is accomplished.**
Quiet music is played and then other voices are heard.

1. It is accomplished?

2. But what is accomplished?

3. What can any man accomplish, nailed to a cross?

1. He speaks as though he has taken over.

2. As though he were already in control.

3. He hangs on a cross and speaks as though it were a throne.

4. As though he were completely in control.

1. Not Pilate.

2. Not Caiaphas.

3. Not the Government.

4. Not the United Nations.

3. Not the Revolution.

1. Somehow he knows that he has accomplished something tremendous.

2. Something tremendous, not just for himself but for all the world.

3 If I could understand what he has accomplished I feel I would understand all the mystery of life.

~ 54 ~   *Credo*

4.   If only I could understand what he has accomplished

2.   If only I could understand.

Voice of Jesus.   **Father into your hands I commit my spirit.**

After a pause with further music, two players meet, one carrying a robe.

First   His?

Second   His!

First   How did you get it?

Second   It was my lucky day, while we were waiting for him to die we threw for it.

First   And you won?

Second   Twice I threw a double six... I'll remember this day. Oh yes, I'll remember this day.

Further music which fades as the Narrator speaks.

Narrator   So you can laugh at this story if you like, laugh, or cry, because, so the tale goes, One Friday in Eternity, God wasn't out there somewhere far beyond the Milky Way; he was hanging on a cross, Just outside Jerusalem.

From the play 'One Friday In Eternity'.
Note. 'It is accomplished' is the translation of John 19:30 given in the REB. Others have 'It is finished'.
The New Jerusalem Bible reads 'It is fulfilled'.

Fighting and Fears

Chapter 5

Resurrection!

And as for the resurrection of the dead, have you not read what was said to you by God, 'I am the God of Abraham, the God of Isaac, and the God of Jacob'? He is God not of the dead, but of the living.
(Matthew 22:31-32 NRSV)

If for this life only we have hoped in Christ, we are of all people most to be pitied. But in fact Christ has been raised from the dead.
(1 Corinthians 15:19,20 NRSV)

- **The Roman Governor gives a press conference**
- **The reality of the cross**
- **An outrageous claim – unless…**
- **On the edge of the unknown**
- **A shatteringly new perspective**
- **'I believe in the resurrection of the body and the life everlasting'**
- **Resurrection now!**
- **A living Lord!**
- **At the Communion Table**
- **So what is Plan B?**

Resurrection!

The Roman Governor gives a press conference

Officer	His Excellency, the Governor!
Pilate	Good morning gentlemen. I can spare just a few minutes. As you put your questions I would be obliged if you would indicate which paper it is that you represent.
First Reporter	Tuscan Times, my Lord Pilate. Would you care to comment on the effectiveness of the security arrangements for the festival?
Pilate	I haven't been able to study the reports of all the Centurions in detail yet, but speaking generally, I am quite satisfied. Everything appears to have gone as peacefully as one could have hoped.
Second Reporter	Jerusalem Echo! Will your Excellency be staying many more days in the Holy City?
Pilate	No longer than I can help, *(mild laughter)* You must remember that the seat of government is in Caesarea
Third Reporter	Caesarea Gazette, your Excellency! What would you say to the suggestion that the release of Barabbas was a sign of weakness?
Pilate	*(with a slight hint of menace)* I wonder who makes the suggestion, it is the first that I have heard of it. The release of the prisoner Barabbas was, as you well know, in accordance with precedent. If Barabbas, or anyone else for that matter, thinks it was a sign of weakness and mounts another challenge to the government they will soon see who is weak and who is strong.

Resurrection!

Fourth Reporter	Rome Courier! Is it true, my Lord Pilate, that the body of Jesus of Nazareth was stolen while the guard slept?
Pilate	If it was, it is no concern of the Government. No Roman soldier was posted to guard a dead criminal. We have quite enough to do dealing with the live ones *(mild laughter)*. However, I suggest that you address your enquiries to the authorities of the national church who have, I believe, an interest in the matter.
Fifth Reporter	Athens Mercury! What have you to say, your Excellency, to the claim that this Jesus of Nazareth has risen from the dead and has been seen in Jerusalem?
Pilate	I should be most happy to meet him if he could spare the time, but he has not so far appeared to me, or, I dare say, to any of you? ... Precisely! And now gentlemen, if you will excuse me ...
Officer	Way for his Excellency the Governor! *(As the reporters hurry off we hear odd snatches of conversation).* Sounds confident enough ... Knew it couldn't have been the Roman guard ... Bit touchy about Barabbas don't you think? ... See you at the Bull, don't be late ... *(and then, loud and clear)* ... Risen from the dead! It'll all be forgotten in a week!

From the play 'One Friday in Eternity'

Resurrection!

The reality of the cross

'Why do you look for the living among the dead? He is not here, but has risen.' Now it was Mary Magdalene, Joanna, Mary the mother of James, and the other women with them who told this to the apostles. But these words seemed to them an idle tale, and they did not believe them. (Luke 24:5,10,11 NRSV)

Few would dispute
the reality of the cross;
oppression, torture and violent death
are all too familiar,
it is the resurrection that poses the problem.

The old myths have been exploded,
heaven is no longer 'out there'.
God has vanished in an ever expanding universe
and only the cross is real,
the devil's answer to our finest dreams.

That day outside Jerusalem
the cross did indeed appear
to be the final word.
Even the disciples of Jesus disbelieved
until they could no longer not believe
and then, in amazement,
they found their lives transformed
by the presence of the Lord they had seen crucified,
living, risen from the dead!

> *Lord, amid our doubts and uncertainties,*
> *our fears and our hesitations,*
> *help us to hold on to the truth*
> *that you are risen,*
> *living with us now,*
> *and that nothing can separate us from your love.*

Resurrection!

An outrageous claim - unless...

God was in Christ, reconciling the world unto himself.
(2 Corinthians 5:19 AV)

That 'God was in Christ reconciling the world to himself',
is an outrageous claim,
unless, of course,
it is true!
But, if it is true,
it changes our whole view of life.

The Christian story
started from the crucifixion and resurrection
of Jesus of Nazareth.
To some the risen Christ was a physical presence,
though appearing and disappearing at will.
To Paul he came as a vision of the road to Damascus.
The resurrection stories are fragmentary
and disjointed;
but who could find words
to adequately express the reality
behind such mind shattering experiences?

Later,
looking back,
those who had been with Jesus realised
that in his daily living
they had seen as much of the nature of God
as human beings could ever understand,
and from then on,
trying to respond to that revelation
mattered more than life itself.

> *Amazing, seeking, reconciling God,*
> *despite all the evil we have done*
> *you have never written us off as worthless.*
> *Glory be to your Holy Name.*

Resurrection!

On the edge of the unknown

I came that they might have life, and have it abundantly.
(John 10:10 NRSV)

On Easter morning we stand
on the edge of the unknown.

Is our time on earth
a matter of chance or of purpose?
Is there really a God
and if so, what sort of God?
- An unpredictable God, needing to be sweetened
  by carefully arranged ceremonies?
- A God of wrath with a rather short fuse?
- A God, however well meaning,
  who, standing back, is no longer in control of events?

Or can we believe in the God proclaimed at Easter,
the God of life triumphing over death?
- Life, for those to whom the devil has whispered
  the lie that they don't matter to a single soul.
- Life for those who have become appalled
  at the depth of evil in their own heart.
- Life for the terminally ill.
- Life as a renewing force.
- Life with new quality, new hope.
- Life which nothing can destroy!

In all these things we are more than conquerors through him who loved us. For I am convinced that neither death, nor life, nor angels, nor rulers, nor things present, nor things to come, nor powers, nor height, nor depth, nor anything else in all creation, will be able to separate us from the love of God in Christ Jesus our Lord.
(Romans 8:37-39 NRSV)

Risen Lord, may that life
which flows from you,
and which not even death can destroy,
be ours now and forever.

A shatteringly new perspective

For as yet they did not understand the scripture, that he must rise from the dead.

(John 20:9 NRSV)

They could never have argued
from the scriptures to the resurrection;
it wasn't the discovery of proof texts
which led them to believe,
but the inescapable fact of the resurrection
which caused them to read the scriptures in a fresh light
and understand the scriptures in a completely new way.

They now knew, as they had never known before,
that the word of God will not be silenced,
the light of God cannot be extinguished,
the love of God recognises no defeat
and the life which flows from God is stronger than death.

It was a shattering experience
which radically changed their lives,
and it can be a shattering experience for us;
for the risen Christ turns upside down
many of the assumptions
on which our lives have been based
and challenges us to really take seriously
the testimony of the scriptures
and face up to the full implications of resurrection.

> *Christ is alive – live confidently!*
> *Christ is alive – live lovingly!*
> *Go to the needy poor*
> *and to the needy rich*
> *and take the message that because Christ lives*
> *neither evil nor death can have the final word.*

'I believe in the resurrection of the body and the life everlasting'

(The Apostles' Creed)

It is sown a physical body, it is raised a spiritual body.
(1 Corinthians 15:44 NRSV)

The resurrection of the body!
But who wants a worn-out body?
Who wants to carry into eternity
rheumatism and arthritis,
corns and bunions,
wheezles and sneezles
and all other ills that flesh is heir to?

The problem lies in the limitations of language.
Other words might suggest
something shadowy, insubstantial,
whereas 'I believe in the resurrection of the body'
affirms a faith in the resurrection
of the whole person,
the real 'me'.

It affirms the faith that beyond death
lies a whole new dimension of living. –
A new creation!
Yet one which might prove strangely familiar
to those who have something of eternity
already planted in their hearts.

> *Loving Saviour,*
> *we pray that you will so deal with us*
> *as we live day by day,*
> *that when the time comes for us*
> *to pass through death*
> *we may be ready to enter into*
> *that new dimension of living, which awaits us,*
> *fit to become part of your new creation.*

Resurrection now!

If anyone is in Christ, there is a new creation. (2 Corinthians 5:17 NRSV)

It is a mistake to think that the resurrection faith
is meant to reconcile us to present miseries
with promises of 'pie in the sky';
on the contrary,
it is a faith which should stimulate us
to live to transform this present time.

When in writing to the church in Corinth
Paul set out his great affirmation of the resurrection faith,
he didn't finish with
'so sit back and wait for the happy ending';
but with,
'Therefore, my beloved,
be steadfast, immovable,
always excelling in the work of the Lord,
because you know that in the Lord
your labour is not in vain.
Now concerning the collection...' [1]

Nor did the early church
get in a huddle around the harmonium singing,
'O that will be, glory for me' –
they went out and proclaimed the living Christ
and found, somewhat to their surprise,
that in the process
they had made quite an impact
upon the life of the society in which they lived.

> *Crucified and risen Lord,*
> *help us to grow closer to you,*
> *that we may reflect in our living*
> *more of the joy and the power*
> *which flows from your living presence among us.*

(1) 1 Corinthians 15:58ff NRSV The collection referred to here was for famine relief, to help people they had never met who were in deep distress. Today Paul might well have written, 'Now concerning Christian Aid Week'

Resurrection!

A living Lord!

Do not be afraid; I am the first and the last, and the living one. I was dead, and see, I am alive forever and ever, and I have the keys of Death and of Hades. (Revelation 1:17,18 NRSV)

But why didn't the risen Christ
return to confront Pilate and Caiaphas,
or those who had stood mocking at the foot of the cross?
why did he only come to those ready to welcome him?

The God who meets us in Jesus
does not compel unwilling allegiance.
The living Lord comes
to those who feel the burden of evil,
not least the evil in their own hearts,
and who long to be delivered from its grasp.

He comes
to those who know the emptiness of life
lived with self at the centre;
and who are aware of how death
mocks all human striving and attainment.

He comes
to those weary of pain
or overwhelmed by grief and sorrow.

And all,
as they become aware of his presence,
know again that without him life has little meaning
and that with him death is not to be feared.

> *Worthy is the Lamb that was slain*
> *to receive power, and riches.*
> *and wisdom, and strength,*
> *and honour, and glory, and blessing.*
>
> *(Revelation 5:12 AV)*

At the Communion Table

For I received from the Lord what I also handed on to you, that the Lord Jesus on the night when he was betrayed took a loaf of bread, and when he had given thanks, he broke it and said, 'This is my body that is for you. Do this in remembrance of me.' In the same way he took the cup also, after supper, saying, 'This cup is the new covenant in my blood. Do this, as often as you drink it, in remembrance of me.' For as often as you eat this bread and drink the cup, you proclaim the Lord's death until he comes.

(1 Corinthians 11:23-26 NRSV)

Crucified and risen Lord,
you call us to be loving, caring people,
putting the needs of others before our own,
reflecting your way of life to the world.
Often we fail you through timidity,
shortsightedness,
or sheer lack of faith
that your way really does work

Forgive us when we fail to live
as fully as we might.
Forgive us when we think more of our disabilities
than of our possibilities.
Forgive us when we allow self pity,
fears, bitterness, resentment or sloth
to mar the lives we offer you.
Forgive us and make us whole.

Teach us, we pray, the generosity of spirit,
the humility, the openness
and the reaching out in loving concern,
which should be the mark of your people;
that as we go about our daily living
others may learn that you are indeed a living Lord
and that we are truly your disciples.

Resurrection!

So what is Plan B?

With Jesus crucified
and us scared stiff that we'd be next,
Plan A was pretty obvious.
Lie low until it was safe to sneak away from Jerusalem
and start life afresh somewhere else.

It had been an exhilarating adventure while it lasted,
a real roller coaster ride
despite the tragic ending.
We might even have pictured ourselves
in later years,
the day's work done,
repeating tales of this man
who had such an amazing way with him
and such startling ideas about the kingdom of God.

But Plan A is out!
Jesus has risen from the dead –
yes, there's no doubt about it –
and we shan't be able to sit back
and talk of what might have been,
say,
'But of course, a man ahead of his time',
finish our drink
and go off to bed.

The kingdom is somehow present
here and now
and whilst we remain on earth
there'll be no discharge from its service.

So Plan A is out!
Time to start working on Plan B!

Chapter 6

Transformation Scene

When the day of Pentecost had come, they were all together in one place. And suddenly from heaven there came a sound like the rush of a violent wind, and it filled the entire house where they were sitting. Divided tongues, as of fire, appeared among them, and a tongue rested on each of them. All of them were filled with the Holy Spirit...
(Acts 2:1-4 NRSV)

And then the king and all estates went home to Camelot, and so went to evensong to the great minister, and so after upon that to supper, and every knight sat in his own place as they were toforehand. Then anon they heard crackling and crying of thunder, that they thought the place should all to drive. In the midst of this blast entered a sunbeam more clearer by seven times than ever they saw day, and all they were alighted of the grace of the Holy Ghost. Then began every knight to behold other, and either saw other, by their seeming, fairer than ever they saw afore.
(Thomas Malory, Le Morte d'Arthur)

- **How long, O Lord, how long?**
- **Beginning at Pentecost**
- **Fruit of the Spirit**
- **A spiritual awakening**
- **A matter of doing the right thing**
- **Private enterprise transformed**
- **A mission to heal**
- **Be an angel!**
- **Not only an angel – be a saint!**
- **Cry to the winds**

Transformation Scene

How long O Lord, how long?

Four people are talking together when another, Angelo, approaches...

Three   There's someone coming!

One   At this hour?

Two   I don't like meeting new people.

Three   He's carrying a torch; it's giving a very good light.

Four   *(Who has almost dozed off)* You going? Oh, a very good night to you.

Three   Not good night! Wash your ears out! There's a man coming with a torch, can't you see him?

Four   I say! Isn't it lovely! I wish I had one.

Angelo   *(entering)* Why not?

Four   You mean that I could have one?

Angelo   The flame is to be shared.

Two   With anybody?

Three   There'll be a charge of course, there is sure to be a charge. Even when it says, 'Send no money now', you always have to pay later.

Angelo   There is no charge.

Three   I don't like the sound of this at all. There's something fishy about it. You don't get anything for nothing in this world. Now tell us straight, where did you get it?

Transformation Scene

Angelo	It was given to me at the border.
One	The border?
Two	Which border?
Three	I thought so! It's foreign!
One	Is it foreign?
Angelo	It was given to me at the border where time meets eternity.
Four	That sounds lovely, I don't understand it of course, but it sounds lovely.
One	D'you know, I think I would like to share the flame.
Two	And so would I.
Three	I give up, I really do! There you go, rushing into things you know nothing about. 'Got it at the border where time meets eternity'. What is that supposed to mean?
Angelo	Have you ever stood on the threshold of eternity? *(It is obvious that she hasn't)* I found myself there with a deep longing in my heart, suddenly I heard a voice, 'Will you carry the undying flame back to humanity? and I found myself saying, 'I will'. But I didn't know where to find the flame or how to carry it, so I stood wondering what I should do when the voice spoke again, 'You have a torch, lift it up', and I found I had got a torch though I'd never noticed it before. So I took the torch and held it up and suddenly it was alight.
Four	Why look, I've got a torch! I often wondered what this was, but of course, it is a torch!

Credo

Transformation Scene

Three	Put that away for goodness sake! Why, you don't even know whether it is safe.
Angelo	Safe? If you mean, is it completely predictable? Can you be sure of controlling it? The answer is no, it is not safe. No flame that comes from the threshold of eternity can be safe.
Three	You see what I mean.
One	If we find our torches and you light them, how do we keep them alight?
Two	Yes, what do we do for fuel?
Angelo	That is both the easiest and the hardest thing of all. Whenever your torch burns low you just hold it high, exposed to the winds of heavens, and it renews itself.
One	For ever?
Angelo	For ever.
Four	Would you light my torch?
One	I think I have one...
Two	And so have I...
Three	There you go again! I'm not against you having lighted torches, indeed I will probably have one myself as a gesture of solidarity; but if we are going to do this thing at all at least let us do it properly. We must form a committee...

(and the committee is formed and decides to accept the flame, but for safety's sake to contain it in a fireplace. As the play develops however, it becomes clear that the flame cannot be contained)

From 'The Flame' a play about the Holy Spirit

Transformation Scene

Beginning at Pentecost

All of them were filled with the Holy Spirit. (Acts 2:4 NRSV)

Repent, and be baptised every one of you in the name of Jesus Christ so that your sins may be forgiven; and you will receive the gift of the Holy Spirit. For the promise is for you, for your children, and for all who are far away, everyone whom the Lord our God calls to him.
(Acts 2:38-39 NRSV)

Filled with the Holy Spirit!
Aware that their sins had been forgiven!
Yes –
but they didn't became perfect overnight,
nor did they always
see eye to eye
in the days that followed.

Yet there's no denying what they achieved,
those men –
yes, and women too,
even though they don't get
as much mention as they might –
who were filled with the Holy Spirit at Pentecost.

The impact they had on the world
is a constant reminder
that a 'spiritual person'
is not one with all the stuffing knocked out of them,
but one with a whole lot of new stuffing added.

> *We pray that through the gift of the Holy Spirit,*
> *we may be equipped*
> *to live each day more positively,*
> *more lovingly,*
> *more able to grapple with the challenge*
> *of being your people in the everyday round*
> *of the world as it actually is.*

Transformation Scene

Fruit of the Spirit

If I speak in the tongues of mortals and of angels, but do not have love, I am a noisy gong or a clanging cymbal. (1 Corinthians 13:1 NRSV)

Now there are varieties of gifts, but the same Spirit, and there are varieties of services, but the same Lord. (1 Corinthians 12:4 NRSV)

A rushing mighty wind,
tongues of fire,
and the breaking of the language barrier!
A great release of power
and tremendous excitment
marked the gift of the Spirit at Pentecost;
but that doesn't mean
that every Spirit filled Christian
will be found jumping up and down
shouting 'Praise the Lord'.

Some, led by the Spirit,
have a charisma manifested
through an adventurous exuberance;
others, led by the same Spirit,
go unobtrusively about the Lord's business;
but all,
if truly led by the Spirit of God,
will show something of the fruit of the Spirit in their lives

The fruit of the Spirit is love, joy, peace, patience, kindness, generosity, faithfulness, gentleness and self control.
(Galatians 5:22,23 NRSV)

> *Heavenly Father, you know my weaknesses even better than I know them myself. Help me, I pray, to resist the selfish and evil impulses which so easily could dominate my life, and so fill me with your Spirit that I may grow to show more of love, joy, peace, patience, kindness, generosity, faithfulnesss and self control in my living day by day.*

Transformation Scene

A spiritual awakening

For I have set you an example, that you also should do as I have done to you. (John 13:15 NRSV)

Wherefore Christian was left to tumble in the Slough of Despond alone...but I beheld in my dream, that a man came to him, whose name was Help, and asked him what he did there? Sir, said Christian, I was bid to go this way by a man called Evangelist, who directed me to yonder gate...and as I was going thither I fell in here... Then, said he, Give me thy hand: so he gave him his hand, and he drew him out, and set him upon firm ground, and bid him go on his way. (John Bunyan 'The Pilgrim's Progress')

Deep in the mud,
struggling ineffectively to keep on the right side
of a taskmaster called 'God',
there can come a moment of joyous spiritual awakening
when the truth suddenly dawns
that God isn't sitting back 'up there'
marking up our sins,
but is down here,
in the mud beside us,
helping us to find a way out.

God the policeman
waiting to pounce;
God the banker
confronting us with an enormous overdraft;
these and other like images
can be thrown overboard.
God the Saviour's love has flooded our hearts;
set free to live, we have passed from death to life.

> *Lord, never let me forget that being spiritual
> isn't so much a matter of keeping myself
> free from stain, as one of looking for others
> who have fallen in the mire
> that I may reach out to give them a helping hand.*

Credo

Transformation Scene

A matter of doing the right thing

We want to get it right!
Should we have bishops?
Who may celebrate the Holy Communion?
What about baptism?
And what should we be careful to avoid
in our day to day living?
These are only a few of the many questions
for which we require answers
if we are to know and live by the rules!

He has told you, O mortal, what is good; and what does the Lord require of you: but to do justice, and to love kindness, and to walk humbly with your God. (Micah 6:8 NRSV)

Does that mean we're starting in the wrong place, Lord?
If Micah is right,
and you aren't too concerned
about our rules and regulations;
should we stop worrying
that people find varying answers
to the questions we are asking?

You shall love the Lord your God with all your heart, and with all your soul, and with all your mind. This is the greatest and first commandment, And a second is like it: You shall love your neighbour as yourself. (Matthew 22:37-39 NRSV)

That before all else?
Is it really as simple –
is it really as hard as that?

> Discerning Spirit, help me to distinguish between
> the important and the unimportant,
> to choose wisely,
> and to judge others as lovingly,
> as I believe God in Christ judges me.

Transformation Scene

Private enterprise transformed

Let each of you look not to your own interests, but to the interests of others. Let the same mind be in you that was in Christ Jesus…
(Philippians 2:4-5 NRSV)

It was private enterprise,
which first established schools
where the poor might learn to read and write
despite the disapproval of those who felt
this was giving people ideas above their station.
It was private enterprise
which struggled for more than a generation
in the teeth of fierce opposition
to end the slave trade.
It was private enterprise
which fought for factory and mine legislation,
established hospitals
and laid the foundation of our welfare services.

Private enterprise
established and sustains
Christian Aid, Cafod, Tear Fund and kindred charities;
a private enterprise which is the very opposite
of everyone seeking their own profit
and the devil take the hindmost.
Private enterprise transformed by the Holy Spirit!
Private enterprise focussed on
laying another brick or two
in the building on earth of some hint
of what the Kingdom of God is like.

> *May the words of my mouth,*
> *the desires of my heart,*
> *and the work of my hands,*
> *all be acceptable in thy sight*
> *my Lord and my Redeemer.*

Transformation Scene

A mission to heal

*Heal the sick, raise the dead, cleanse lepers, drive out demons.
You received without cost; give without charge.* (Matthew 10:8 REB)

A healing ministry!
Not one replacing the skills
of physician, surgeon, nurse or therapist;
but a ministry reaching out lovingly
where their skills may be of little avail.

Patiently listening;
quietly sharing the pain of sorrow or grief;
seeking to open channels
through which the Holy Spirit may bring
wholeness to lives broken or incomplete,
to lives where,
however healthy the outward appearance,
there is dis-ease.

To be healers we must first be lovers.
Even thought we may disapprove
of the one who needs us;
even though we may find them intensely irritating;
we can learn to listen to their concerns,
to care for their welfare,
and to pray for their well being.
From such beginnings,
who knows what the Lord may do?

> *Lord Jesus Christ,
> we pray for healing that we may be healers;
> we pray for blessing that we may bring blessing to others;
> We pray we may glimpse the kingdom in our midst
> that we may truly be able to declare,
> 'Rejoice!, The kingdom of God is at hand'.*

We must never forget that some of the
greatest of God's servants have had a
hard struggle against sickness or
disability; yet, often enough, this is the
very reason that they have been so
effective. There are times when we
recognise 'wholeness' despite
physical weakness. The glory of God
shines through an inner spirit which is
radiantly alive.

*A Thorn was given me in the flesh,
a messanger of Satan to torment me,
to keep me from being too elated.
Three times I appealed to the Lord about this,
That it would leave me, but he said to me,
"my grace is sufficient for you, for power is
made perfect in weakness."*
                            (2 Corinthians 12. 7-9 NRSV)

Transformation Scene

Be an angel!

You use the winds as your messengers and flashes of lightening as your servants. (Psalm 104:4 GNB)

God makes his angels winds, and his servants flames of fire.
(Hebrews 1:7 GNB)

No wings are required
by 21st century angels;
they will walk, cycle,
travel by bus, train or car,
and should they need to fly,
they will use a plane.

The call to be angels,
– messengers,
– witnesses,
in the power which the Spirit gives,
is one that comes to all God's people –

'God makes his angels winds'.
Just as God breathed into Adam the breath of life [1]
so we are called to be instruments
through which the breath of life may flow
to renew our community.

'And his servants flames of fire'.
As the worker in precious metals uses fire for refining
and the gardener's bonfire produces valuable potash;
so we are meant to become channels
for the refining, stimulating
work of the Holy Spirit in the world.

> Lord, of our yesterdays, our today and our tomorrows
> let your Spirit so flow in us
> that we may become worthy to be your angels,
> and able to share in your work in our world.

(1) Genesis 3:8

Transformation Scene

Not only an angel – be a saint!

To the church of God that is in Corinth...called to be saints.
(1 Corinthians 1,2 NRSV)

They were called to be saints
in Corinth, Ephesus, Philippi, Antioch, Rome...
indeed, wherever the church was to be found.
Just ordinary men and women
facing ordinary human problems.
No halos!
No whiter than white clothes!
They weren't unworldly beings
living in stained glass windows,
but down to earth folks who,
had they lived today,
might have been found
unblocking a drain,
pushing a shopping trolley,
getting the children off to school
or feeding the cat.
They were called to be part of the worshipping community,
living out their faith as best they could
and sometimes making quite a mess of it;
yet, by the Grace of God,
never giving up.

So don't wait for the Pope
or anybody else to make it official;
they were called to be saints and so are we.
Be a saint,
now!

> *Are you sure you mean me, Lord?*
> *I don't feel very saintly,*
> *but, with your help for my living*
> *and your forgiveness for my failures,*
> *I'll try,*
> *I really will.*

Transformation Scene

Cry to the winds

Cry to the winds,
blow free, blow free;
cry to the flame,
to be, to be;
grasp the torch and hold it high
let it dance against the sky;
cry to the winds,
blow free, blow free.

Cry to the winds
renew, renew
cry to the earth,
be true, be true,
fan the spark into a flame
make the fire burn again,
cry to the winds
renew, renew.

Angelo's song.
From 'The Flame' a play about the Holy Spirit

In a world of plenty,
some have far more wealth than they can use
while others exist in abject poverty.
Some have food enough and to spare
while others die of hunger.
Some take comfortable homes for granted
while others eke out their existence
in insanitary hovels.

Spirit of the Living God,
so stir us that we may never accept
that such situations should exist unchallenged.
Wherever we may be able to serve
those who have little of this world's goods
make us ready to be used as channels of your love.

Chapter 7

People of God ?

Listen! I am standing at the door, knocking; if you will hear my voice and open the door, I will come in to you and eat with you, and you with me. To the one who conquers I will give a place with me on my throne, just as I myself conquered and sat down with my Father on his throne. Let any one who has an ear listen to what the Spirit is saying to the churches.
(Revelation 3:21,22 NRSV)

'Went to church today,' wrote Robert Louis Stevenson in his journal, 'and was not greatly depressed.'

Now here, you see, it takes all the running you can do, to keep in the same place. If you want to get somewhere else, you must run at least twice as fast as that!
(Lewis Carroll 'Alice Through The looking Glass')

- **An answer to prayer**
- **A true high churchmanship**
- **Part of the Body of Christ**
- **Born again Christians**
- **Not a religion, but a way**
- **The church where we worship**
- **The stories that count**
- **One church, one faith, one Lord**
- **Two prayers for the people of God**

An answer to prayer

We find three people together who are unexpectedly joined by a fourth.

One	Do you think we've come to the right place?
Two	This is where he said.
One	I know, but somehow it doesn't feel right.
Three	It's them he should be focussing on, people at the top, not us. It's no good expecting anything of us. It's up to them to do something.
Two	Something about the homeless for a start.
Three	And the old people.
Two	And crime. It gets worse every year.
Three	We need better roads
Two	Better schools.
Three	Better...
One	*(with a change of tone)* This is the hour of prayer.
Two	Already?
Three	Doesn't time fly?
One	I said, this is hour of prayer.
Three	We heard.
One	Then let us pray
All	For what we are about the receive, may the Lord make us truly thankful. Aaa-men!

People of God ?

Four	*(Who suddenly appears after a short pause)* Hi there!
One	Who are you?
Four	I'm it. What you've been praying for. I'm the answer.
Three	What d'you mean you're the answer? We were only praying. We weren't expecting anything.
One	We've never had an answer before.
Four	Well, you've got one now. For what you were about to receive. You've received me.
Three	Who are you anyway?
Four	I'm your guardian angel.
Three	Guardian angel! You've been a long time coming. Well, since you are here, what are you going to do for us?
Four	Nothing!
One,Two,Three	Nothing?
Three	Not much point in coming if you are going to do anything
Four	But I am. I'm bringing you a message.
Two	What sort of message?
Four	It's about your prayer. The Almighty sent me to say that he's very glad to know you are so concerned about what is wrong in the world.
Three	That's nice of him.
Two	That wasn't our prayer.

Credo

People of God ?

One	He must have been listening to our conversation.
Two	So he's glad we are concerned. But what's he going to do about it?
Four	The Almighty says if you'll just pray, 'Lord, show me how to help you in the world?', he'll be delighted to provide a few openings.
Three	He's not going to do anything!
One	*(After a pause)* I was brought up to be one of his supporters and I've done my bit, Christmas, Easter, never failed. I really don't think it's good enough. I'm hurt, very hurt. Exits
Two	It's come to something now if you can't pray without the risk of being asked to do something. I wouldn't have credited it. I've prayed all my life till now, but if this is going to happen I shall seriously consider taking up Yoga instead, and you can tell him when you see him. Exits
Three	It's not that I wouldn't like to be helpful, but you see, you've really got the wrong people, it's not us you want...
Four	*(Finishing it)* It's them!
Three	See you again some time?
Four	That's up to you. *(Three Exits. Four turns to audience)* Well folks, it goes for you as well you know. The Lord will be delighted to hear of any offers of service, absolutely delighted. Call him any time – freephone – the lines are open twenty four hours.

(Abbreviated from the sketch 'Them and Us' in 'A Fistful of Fivers')

A true high churchmanship

To him who by means of his power working in us is able to do so much more than we can ever ask for, or even think of: to God be glory in the church... (Ephesians 3:20-21 GNB)

Here is a miracle!
Crazy mixed up creatures that we are,
the eternal God calls us
to share in the saving work of Christ.
The Almighty is prepared to deal with us,
to use us, even, at times, to wait for us.

But do we really believe this?
Do we dare to hold this high church position,
which is our inheritance?
High churchmanship!
Not depending on particular forms or ceremonies,
not depending on particular dress or ritual,
but high churchmanship grounded in the fact
that we really do believe in the church;
that we really do believe
that in and through Jesus Christ,
God not only calls us,
but enables us to be his witnesses,
calls us and empowers us
to embody the hope of the world;

> *Almighty God, what have we to bring you*
> *but our weakness and our awareness of inadequacy?*
> *Help us to rise above our fears and our doubts,*
> *to rise above our petty pride and self interest,*
> *let your love possess us,*
> *and flow through us so strongly*
> *that we may really give glory to you,*
> *both in our worship*
> *and in the way we go about our daily living.*

People of God?

Part of the Body of Christ

All of you are Christ's body, and each one is a part of it.
(1 Corinthians 12:27 GNB)

If we are to be part of the body of Christ
there can be no room for
standing on our dignity,
no room for
personal rivalries,
no room for
denominational idiosyncrasies.
If we are really to be part of the body of Christ
we must try to live as he lived.

Our Lord was accessible
and, being accessible, vulnerable.
Even when he needed quiet
people pressed in on him;*
his living was totally for others.
To make others whole
his body was broken;
indeed,
we have to face the fact
that there is no way
we can truly be part of the body of Christ
without sooner or later
ourselves getting hurt.

> *But he was pierced for our transgressions,*
> *crushed for our iniquities;*
> *the chastisement he bore restored us to health*
> *and by his wounds we are healed.*
> *(Isaiah 53:5 REB)*

People of God?

*(Jesus) said to them, 'Come away to a deserted place all by yourselves and rest awhile.' For many were coming and going, and they had no leisure even to eat... Now many saw them going and recognised them, and they hurried there on foot from all the towns and arrived ahead of them. As he went ashore, he saw a great crowd; and he had compassion for them ...

(Mark 6:31-34 NRSV)

People of God ?

Born again Christians

You have been born anew, not of perishable but of imperishable seed, through the living and enduring word of God. (1 Peter 1:23 NRSV)

To an infant
all is wonder and fresh experience;
but growing older
we are not so open to new, startling ideas,
unless we are born again
to the inquiring,
wondering approach to life
which is the mark of the very young.

An infant is of necessity
dependent
and so comes to trust
the one who supplies its needs.
Being born again
means for us
learning what it really means
to put our whole trust in God.

Just as an infant
has no memory of the past to weigh it down,
so new life in Christ
means letting go past failures
and rebirth to a new start.
This is surely the greatness
of the promise of the forgiveness of sins;
the weight is taken from us
and we are set free to live

> *Lord, help me to know my need*
> *and, as a young child trusts a loving parent,*
> *to trust that I am held in your love*
> *and to live in the confidence*
> *that nothing can take that love from me.*

Not a religion, but a way

Jesus said, I am the way, the truth and the life... I will never turn away anyone who comes to me. (John 16:6 & 6:37 GNB)

Religions have a way of being exclusive.
You are vetted, prepared and initiated
and then you are 'in',
you are 'different', you have 'made it'.

The Pharisees drew very clear lines
between those who were the people of God
and those who were not
and unfortunately
something of the same understanding of 'religion'
still permeates the Christian church.
Yet Christianity isn't really a religion –
it's a faith,
it's a way,
a way to be taken
by anybody and everybody.

A real church is not,
and never can be a 'closed shop'.
Christ's invitation is to 'whomsoever will'.
And so the more the church,
any church,
is true to its calling,
the more it will be open to all comers –
whatever the risk!

> *Lord, strengthen my will to*
> *follow you, who are the way*
> *and to heed you, who are the truth*
> *that I may be filled with you, who are the life.*

People of God ?

The church where we worship

If you have ears, then, listen to what the Spirit says to the churches.
(Revelation 2:7 GNB)

That church where we worship –
is it a happy fellowship of like minded souls
with whom for a while
we can retreat from the world
in order to get topped up
to meet the demands
of yet another hectic week?

Or is that local church,
with all its human frailties,
a resource
for the Living Christ
to take and use
in reaching out to the world
for which he lived,
and died
and rose again?

What do we seek?
A well established rest-centre for the weary?
Or a forward base for a unit on active service?

> *Lord of the church,*
> *may we find the renewal we seek*
> *in a loving fellowship*
> *within our local congregation;*
> *but may we also be a people*
> *reaching out to proclaim your Good News,*
> *in word and deed*
> *to the world beyond our walls.*

Many of the people
you and I will meet outside the church
are still nominal Christians
who, deep down,
are sorry that the fire
has burnt so low.
Fire rekindles fire!

Numbers have little to do with it.
A handful of people
can be really waiting,
really listening,
really afire.
A large congregation
careful not to stand up too soon
or sing too loudly
are defeated from the start.

Even the Holy Spirit
can hardly be expected
to kindle a fire in a refrigerator.

People of God ?

The stories that count

When a dog bites a man that is not news, but when a man bites a dog that is news. (The New York Sun 1882)

The Kingdom of God is like this. A man scatters seed in his field. He sleeps at night, is up and about during the day, and all the while the seeds are sprouting and growing. Yet he does not know how it happens.
(Mark 4:26-27 GNB)

Don't worry if you go unreported!

The daily round of ordinary
decent people
isn't news;
yet it is in the everyday struggle
to live honestly,
compassionately,
creatively,
lovingly,
that the great stories of life are written.

Such stories seldom make the news;
but it is these
unsensational,
unreported stories,
these
hidden
holy stories,
that are the building bricks
of the Kingdom of God.

>Grant to me, Lord, I pray,
>the understanding that can delight
>in going quietly about your business;
>doing each day what comes to hand to be done
>and making me glad to be counted
>a servant of your hidden kingdom.

People of God ?

One church, one faith, one Lord

One says, 'I follow Paul'; another, 'I follow Apollos'; another, 'I follow Peter'; and another, 'I follow Christ.' Christ has been divided into groups! (1 Corinthians 1:12,13 GNB)

I can sing, 'Thy hand, O God has guided'
with its refrain, 'One church, one faith, one Lord',
not because I shut my eyes to,
or am unaffected by our divisions,
but because I believe
that the Lord of all Christians,
somehow makes sense of our nonsense.

I believe that it is indeed one church,
because Christ holds us in one body,
however much at times we try to deny it.
And that it is indeed one faith,
though because of our human limitations
we see it from different perspectives,
and have different emphases
when we try to state it.

I believe that I have a duty
to play my part in that section of the church
in which I find myself;
whilst at the same time
working for greater fellowship
and understanding with all Christians
that the 'oneness' of the church
may be less hidden by our insularities.

> Lord Jesus Christ, grant us the humility and the grace
> to recognise your presence
> in church traditions other than our own
> that we may be ready to learn from them
> and so to learn ever more of you.

Two prayers for the people of God

Lord, we pray that you will take hold of us
and make us into a living,
pulsating, vibrant church –
full of fallible humanity,
how could it be otherwise? –
but humanity being moulded and transformed
by its living Lord.
Let us become a church made up of people
ready to take risks,
ready to lose themselves
for the world you loved,
the world for which you gave your all.

Lord, we do want to be part of your body,
help us, we pray,
when the path ahead is obscure.
Help us when we have to grapple
with evil masquerading as good
and with darkness claiming to be light.
Help us, when we are tempted to
pull the blankets over our heads
to shut out the storm,
and remind us that the inner security
which we seek
has to be found in the very heart of the storm.
And when all is going wrong,
as at times it surely will,
and we are tempted to say
'it isn't worth the effort'
remind us again, we pray,
 of your promise
'I will be with you always,
to the end of the age'.

(Matthew 28:20 GNB)

Chapter 8

The Trivial Round

I do not understand my own behaviour; I do not act as I mean to, but I do the things that I hate... What a wretched man I am! Who will rescue me from this body doomed to death? God – thanks be to him – through Jesus Christ our Lord. (Romans 7:15,24-25 NJB)

Then since the gifts that we have differ according to the grace that was given to each of us; if it is a gift of prophecy, we should prophesy as much as our faith tells us; if it is a gift of practical service, let us devote ourselves to serving; if it is teaching, to teaching; if it is encouraging, to encouraging. When you give, you should give generously from the heart; if you are put in charge, you must be conscientious; if you do works of mercy, let it be because you enjoy doing them. Let love be without any pretence. (Romans 12:6-9 NJB)

The trivial round, the common task
would furnish all we ought to ask:
room to deny ourselves, a road
to bring us daily nearer God (John Keble)

- **The eternal Adam**
- **Starting at home**
- **Neighbours!**
- **A proper pride**
- **Part of the action**
- **The years pass and the world changes**
- **Heaven in my heart, but my feet on the ground**
- **Weakness and strength**
- **Technology – old and new**

The Trivial Round

The eternal Adam

Chorus A	Well, that's it.
Chorus B	We've just got time for a brief summing up before the next programme.
Chorus A	What about Adam and Eve, d'you think they did as well as they might have done?
Chorus B	Not at all. Of course, they were novices.
Chorus A	Quite, no experience.
Chorus B	However, there's no two ways about it. The blame for the mess that the world is in lies fairly and squarely on their shoulders.
Chorus A	I'm sure our viewers would agree with that. To put it bluntly, they're responsible for the whole sorry mess.
Chorus B	And if they hadn't eaten the forbidden fruit we should all be living blissfully in Eden.
Chorus A	And with that we must say, goodbye. Next week we shall be looking at Armageddon.
Adam	*(Entering and joining them)* Don't be in such a hurry. We haven't finished yet.
Chorus B	You can't come barging in like this.
Adam	I am here and you cannot put me out because I am a part of you and you are part of me. Bone of my bone, flesh of my flesh.
Chorus B	You've got it all wrong. We are the Chorus.
Chorus A	The commentators.

Adam	You delude yourselves. You live in a world where there are no spectator seats. You are involved *(to audience)* and you and you. You have all eaten of the tree of knowledge, awareness of good and evil are part of your very being.
Chorus B	I like that! It's all your fault that we are shut out from Paradise.
Adam	Paradise? Paradise lies ahead, not behind. Don't imagine that a return to Eden would be a journey to Paradise. The innocence of Eden was primitive and terrible. It was the innocence of infancy, knowing no evil only because it knows no good.
Chorus A	At least in Eden we would have been free from inhibitions and guilt hangovers.
Adam	Free? The freedom of Eden knew no restrictions because it knew no duty. It was completely irresponsible.
Chorus B	I've had enough of this.
Chorus A	Me too. If he won't go then we will.
Adam	Where? Where will you go? You are Adam as I am Adam. We belong to each other and to the earth. Dust of the earth, that's what we are, dust of the earth brought to life by the breath of God.
Chorus B	My good man, there's no need to start getting all theological. We *(The gesture embraces the audience)* are spectators. We are trained spectators. Before ever we can walk we are set in front of a screen to watch the world go by. When the world finally blows up, we'll still be sitting there in our arm chairs watching it.

Adam   You delude yourselves. You may think you are spectators, but you are the event. Eden is part of your experience whether as memory or as dream. Failure and pain and sorrow are part of your own experience, but so are success and pleasure and joy. My gift to you, yes, my gift to you, is that you know good and you know evil and you have the power to choose. You must contend with Cain in your own heart and face the seductions of the tempter, but the breath of the Almighty is in you and if you will listen, you may still hear his voice.

From the One Act Play 'Adam'

Starting at home

So God created humankind in his image, in the image of God he created them; male and female he created them. (Genesis 1:27 NRSV)

Put away from you all bitterness and wrath and anger and wrangling and slander, together with all malice, and be kind to one another, tenderhearted, forgiving one another, as God in Christ has forgiven you. (Ephesians 4:31-32 NRSV)

If marriages are made in heaven
they are only supplied in kits for self assembly;
good marriages are the fruit
of much hard work and mutual caring
on the part of both partners.

As opposed to the desire
to grasp, possess, exploit,
and then,
growing tired,
maybe discard;
true love is constant in caring and giving,
whether it be to wife, husband, partner, parent,
sister, brother, child, or friend.

In surrendering the freedom
to go our own way with little thought for others,
we lay the foundations for stable, joyous relationships.
Human beings are made for community
and none of us can be whole
living for ourselves alone.

> *Lord, save us from taking*
> *those closest to us for granted*
> *and from expecting that they*
> *will always fall in with our wishes.*
> *Save us from expecting them*
> *to tolerate our 'off days'*
> *while never having any of their own.*
> *Lead us, we pray, in the ways of true love.*

The Trivial Round

Neighbours!

This is what love is: it is not that we have loved God, but that he loved us and sent his Son to be the means by which our sins are forgiven. Dear friends, if this is how God loved us, then we should love one another. (1 John 4:10 GNB)

Which, do you think, was a neighbour to the man who fell into the hands of the robbers? (Luke 10:36 NRSV)

God in Christ accepts me, just as I am,
and asks that I in turn
should reach out lovingly to others;
the only problem is
that there are some folks I really can't stand,
folks I find utterly objectionable.

Then I get the uncomfortable thought
that the love of God knows no exceptions,
but goes on caring
even when what it would give
is thrown back in its face.

Well, I know I can't match that,
but it would seem that If I am confronted
with someone with a real need,
a need I could do something about,
then,
without having to approve
their ways of thinking and behaving,
it's up to me to give what help I can
with as much loving concern as I can muster.

> *Lord, give me I pray, the grace*
> *to show in my living something of the love*
> *with which you surround me.*
> *A love which cares and goes on caring,*
> *even through rejection and humiliation,*
> *a love which can never be defeated.*

A proper pride

If anyone else has reason to be confident in the flesh, I have more.
(Philippians 3:4 NRSV)

– we are children of God, and if children, then heirs, heirs of God and joint heirs with Christ – (Romans 8:17 NRSV)

Yes, there is a place for pride!

I'm proud that God loves me
and is ready to trust me
with work to do
during my time here on earth.

I realise
that doesn't
make me better than others;
different maybe,
because we are all unique,
different,
but not better.

And I know it's not enough
just to be proud that God loves me;
it's up to me to try to live in a way
that is a little more worthy of that love.

Of course –
that's
the really hard part.

> Lord, pride is a funny thing,
> and proper pride
> can so easily become something else.
> Help me, I pray, to have a proper pride in myself
> that I may grow closer to what you've created me to be,
> but help me also to value others
> for what you see in them.

Part of the action

...the man who had been possessed by demons begged him that he might be with him. But Jesus refused, and said to him, 'Go home to your friends, and tell them how much the Lord has done for you, and what mercy he has shown you.' (Mark 5:18,19 NRSV)

You will be witnesses for me. (Acts 1:8 GNB)

Strong,
violent,
deranged,
frightenly unpredictable
and living rough among the tombs
of a scared community;
how long would it take for them to accept him back again?
The way would not be easy,
yet restored to his right mind
he would be a powerful witness
to the transforming work of Christ.

Called to be witnesses,
we each
in our own way
have to be part of the action.
Witnesses must testify
to what they have actually experienced,
hearsay is not enough.
We need to show how we ourselves
have been helped, strengthened,
guided,
challenged !
We are called to reveal in our day to day living
how God in Jesus Christ has touched our lives.

> *O Lord,*
> *open thou my lips,*
> *and my mouth*
> *shall show forth your praise*

The years pass and the world changes

When I was a child, I spoke like a child, I thought like a child, I reasoned like a child; when I became an adult, I put an end to childish ways. (1 Corinthians 13:11 NRSV)

I grew up with certain values
and certain ways of doing things
and I never really questioned them.
I grew up in a particular church tradition,
and never doubted that it was the best.

But the years pass and the world changes.
Today my understanding
of what is good or bad,
right or wrong,
is not the same as it was when I was young.
I know this has to be,
but I sometimes wonder
whether all the changes
in the way I think
and in the way I shape my life
have been for the best?
Has anything valuable been lost by the way?

> *Lord, guide me I pray, as I make decisions*
> *about what I should do or not do;*
> *about what I should be holding to*
> *and what I should be letting go.*
> *Remind me, when I need reminding,*
> *that I should not fear change,*
> *but help me also to recognise*
> *the things that do not change*
> *and to cherish and hold to*
> *the values that are eternal.*

The Trivial Round

Heaven in my heart, but my feet on the ground

So, whether you eat or drink, or whatever you do, do everything for the glory of God. (1 Corinthians 10:31 NRSV)

There are moments
when in church,
in the open countryside,
or maybe just sitting quietly at home,
I am able to forget
all the little things demanding attention,
and feel closer
to the kingdom
that is not of this world.

What a gulf there is
between your holiness,
your eternal purposes
and the things that fill my days...

Or is there?

Is it right that I'm to seek you
not so much in withdrawal
as in the ordinary stuff of life,
the trivial round,
the common task
even if some of it is extremely trivial?

> Open my eyes, Lord,
> and strengthen my purpose,
> so that I may indeed find and serve you
> in the little, everyday things of life.
> Let me have heaven in my heart
> but my feet on the ground
> so that I may aim at doing
> even the simplest things to your glory.

Weakness and strength

I saw the Lord... I said, 'There is no hope for me! I am doomed because every word that passes my lips is sinful. (Isaiah 6:1,5 GNB)

It is not always a comfortable experience
to draw nearer to God;
It can make us
far more aware
of the vast gulf that exists
between God's ways and our own.

In the name of God
I need to take a stand against
selfishness, greed, dishonesty. injustice,
violence, oppression...
the list could go on and on;
but the battle only begins
as I wrestle against these very evils
deep in my own heart.*

I am part and parcel of the world I live in.
I am a sinner,
called to bear witness to other sinners,
called to testify to the saving love
of the risen and living Christ
who can still work miracles,
even in me.

> *Renew me, Lord, with the breath of life*
> *touch me with your holy fire*
> *that, despite all my follies,*
> *I may be able to be*
> *part of your mission*
> *of renewal for the world.*

* *David, angrily condemning the rich man who had stolen from his poor neighbour, found, when Nathan said to him, 'You are the man', that he was condemning himself.*

(2 Samuel 12:7)

The Trivial Round

Technology - old and new

Communication has been revolutionised.
Radio, television,
mail shots, recorded messages,
fax, e mail, web sites...
surely these are the ways to make the Gospel known!
And yet –
before we get completely carried away
by modern technology –

The life of Jesus **was** the Gospel.
He cared about people
who were not used
to having others care for them.
He gave himself for others
to the point of utter exhaustion
and for our sakes
he ultimately faced an agonising death.

Jesus showed God as utterly involved in our lives;
suffering with his people
and, when things were at their worst,
turning the situation inside out
to bring victory out of defeat.

Modern technology
is a useful servant,
but in the end
there is no substitute
for actually **living** the Gospel.

Chapter 9
Wider Horizons

Then people will come from east and west, from north and south, and will eat in the kingdom of God.
(Luke13:29 NRSV)

*I dream'd in a dream I saw a city invincible to the attacks
of the whole of the rest of the earth,
I dream'd that was the new city of Friends,
Nothing was greater there than the quality of robust love,
it led the rest,
It was seen every hour in the actions of the men of that city,
And in all their looks and words.*
('I dream'd in a dream' Walt Whitman)

- **Early retirement?**

- **Rights – and responsibilities**

- **The basic stuff of life**

- **A call to share the earth's bounty**

- **'Be biased towards the poor'**

- **Not 'Why did it happen?' but, 'How can I help?'**

- **A vision of peaceful co-existence**

- **God of all peoples?**

- **Living, we must learn to live**

Early retirement?

A soul, newly arrived at heaven's gate,
was warmly greeted by St Peter,
who, turning to the screen in front of him
said,
> 'Well now, let's have a look at your record.
> Baptised, active church member,
> keen supporter of mission and relief work,
> good, good.
> Brought up family,
> played your part in the community,
> excellent, excellent ...'

Then St Peter paused, looked hard at the screen
as if wanting to be sure he'd read it correctly
and said,
> 'But all of a sudden you stopped;
> your very words were, "I've done enough,
> let someone else have a go for a change"'

The new arrival, looking a little sheepish,
was quiet for a while and then replied,
> 'Well, I felt I was entitled to sit back for a year or two'.

'But', cried St Peter,
> 'that was twenty seven years ago
> and what have you done since then?
> Damn all!' [1]

There was another pause, a long one,
then the newcomer spoke:
> 'Was it really as long ago as that?'

Another, even longer pause followed,
at last the newcomer spoke again.
> 'I suppose you could blame
> the National Health Service,
> ..... couldn't you?

---

[1] *A colloquial expression Simon Peter might have picked up in Capernaum after a fruitless fishing session*

Rights - and responsibilities

*The first (commandment) is, 'Hear, O Israel: the Lord our God,
is one; you shall love the Lord your God with all your heart, and with
all your soul, and with all your mind, and with all your strength.
'The second is this, 'You shall love your neighbour as yourself'.*
(Mark 12:30,31 NRSV)

I have my rights!
"Human Rights"
recognised in international law,
and I mean to see that I get them!

What's that, Lord?
I wasn't expecting to hear from you
just at this moment.
No, no; drop by any time you like,
no problem.
Yes, I believe I did mention 'Human Rights',
nothing wrong in that is there?

Responsibilities?
Do we have to bring them in at this moment?
We do? Of course, Lord, if that's how you see it ...
Yes, Lord, I am listening.

Are you really saying that rights and responsibilities
should go hand in hand?
You are! Well, if you say so, Lord –
You do!
Yes, I've got the point ...
I think ...

> *Help me, Lord, to be concerned*
> *for the rights of all peoples,*
> *and let me never forget*
> *that all are held in your love,*
> *especially those*
> *least able to fend for themselves.*

The basic stuff of life

In the morning there was a layer of dew around the camp. When the dew lifted, there on the surface of the wilderness was a fine flaky substance, as fine as frost on the ground. When the Israelites saw it, they said to one another, 'What is it?' For they did not know what it was. Moses said to them, 'It is the bread that the Lord has given you to eat'. (Exodus 16:15 NRSV)

'All stock must be cleared
to make way for fresh deliveries!
Great bargains in all departments!
Buy now!
Nothing to pay – yet!'

But,
forget the market place for a moment,
the basic stuff of life is given,
and given freely.
We can use or abuse,
hallow or desecrate,
but we cannot create,
neither can we possess.

Vast estate or tiny garden,
mansion or terraced house,
we own them for just as long
as God gives breath.
We are at best, stewards,
who one day
must give an account of our stewardship.

> *Lord, forgive us the damage we have done,
> knowingly or unknowingly, to our world
> and the way in which we waste valuable resources.
> Renew, we pray, our sense of wonder
> at the riches of creation.
> and remind us that in every step we take
> we walk on holy ground.*

> Holy is the soil we walk on,
> holy everything that grows,
> holy all beneath the surface,
> holy every stream that flows.

We will learn to share for the joy of sharing,
learn to serve for the joy of serving,
learn to love for the joy of loving,
this is the way of the Lord.

> Holy is the soil we walk on,
> holy everything that grows,
> holy all beneath the surface,
> holy every stream that flows.

We will sing to the Lord for the joy of singing,
give to the Lord for the joy of giving,
live to the Lord for the joy of living,
this is the way of the Lord.

> Holy is the soil we walk on,
> holy everything that grows,
> holy all beneath the surface,
> holy every stream that flows.

From 'The Maker of Things' a light hearted cantata about our place in creation

Wider Horizons

A call to share the earth's bounty

When you have come into the land that the Lord your God is giving you... you shall take some of the first of all the fruit of the ground, which you harvest from the land... and you shall put it in a basket and go to the place that the Lord your God shall choose as a dwelling for his name... Then you, together with the Levites and the aliens who reside among you, shall celebrate with all the bounty that the Lord your God has given...

(Deuteronomy 26:1,2,11 NRSV)

First fruits!
After the privations of winter
the eagerly awaited spring harvest
brought with it the reminder
that it was not to be selfishly hoarded,
but offered back to God by sharing,
not only with family and friends,
but also with those regarded
as rank outsiders.

We still find it hard to accept
that the good things of life
are meant to be shared with the alien,
the asylum seeker, the economic migrant...

An even harder lesson
is that In the kingdom of God
there is no such person as an alien,
there all are made welcome.

> Lord, forgive us
> when we keep the best for ourselves
> and offer you our loose change.
> Forgive us when we are reluctant
> to reach out to those outside our circle
> and show us the joy to be found
> in being open handed
> reflecting in some small measure
> your giving of yourself to us.

'Be biased towards the poor'

When you reap your harvest in your field and forget a sheaf in the field, you shall not go back to get it; it shall be left for the alien, the orphan and the widow, so that the Lord your God may bless you in all your undertakings. (Deuteronomy 24:19 NRSV)

When you give a banquet, invite the poor, the crippled, the lame, and the blind. And you will be blessed, because they cannot repay you, for you will be repaid at the resurrection of the righteous.
(Luke 14:13-14 NRSV)

Generous and loving God,
we thank you for the beauty and the fruitfulness
of the land in which we live
and for the many riches we enjoy
which come to us from other countries.
We thank you that we never need go hungry or thirsty
not knowing where to turn for food or drink.

Save us from taking these gifts for granted.
Stimulate our concern for your needy peoples
who starve in a world of plenty.
Help us to honour you by treating
all men and women, the world over,
as children of the one Heavenly Father,
brothers and sisters for whom Christ died.

Help us, we pray, to grow in loving concern
and instinctive generosity
that we may praise you,
not only in words, but in deeds.
> For thine is the kingdom,
> the power and the glory,
> for ever and ever. Amen

God loves a cheerful giver. And God is able to provide you with every blessing in abundance, so that by always having enough of everything, you may share abundantly in every good work.
(2 Corinthians 9:8 NRSV)

Wider Horizons

Not 'Why did it happen?' but, 'How can I help?'

Those eighteen who were killed when the tower of Siloam fell on them – do you think they were worse offenders than all the others living in Jerusalem? No, I tell you. (Luke 13:4,5 NRSV)

As he walked along, he saw a man blind from birth. His disciples asked him, 'Rabbi, who sinned, this man or his parents, that he was born blind?' Jesus answered, 'Neither this man nor his parents sinned; he was born blind so that God's work might be revealed in him.'
(John 9:1-3 NRSV)

Jesus accepted a world
in which anybody,
good and bad alike,
might suffer disability,
or be suddenly hit by calamity.

A tower collapsed in Siloam
and a number of bystanders were killed.
Jesus firmly rejected the idea
that they had been singled out
as the objects of divine wrath.

And to ask whose fault it was
that a man should be born blind,
was to ask entirely the wrong question.

Ask rather,
'This man with a disability,
this woman with a need;
what can be done to help them?'

> *Show us, Lord, how to look on the need of others,*
> *in whatever form it confronts us,*
> *asking the question*
> *'What does the service of God require of us,*
> *what aid can we offer here?'*

~ 116 ~   Credo

A vision of peaceful co-existence

The wolf shall live with the lamb, the leopard shall lie down with the kid, the calf and the lion and the fatling together. (Isaiah 11:6 NRSV)

The leopard and the young goat
may indeed lie down together,
but it will require
a major change
in lifestyle and expectation
on the part of the leopard
if they are both to be there next morning.

Yet peace, true peace,
enduring peace,
will depend upon the powerful
no longing preying upon the weak.
There can be no peace without justice –
God's justice,
the doing of right by the defenceless.

The aggressive, competitive,
thrusting materialism of our day,
laying heavy burdens
on those least able to bear them,
is in direct conflict with the ways
of our Heavenly Father
and must be vigorously challenged
if the world is ever to know true peace.

> *Teach us, Lord, so to value peace,*
> *true peace, that we become willing*
> *to make the changes necessary*
> *in our own way of living*
> *to achieve a peace that embraces*
> *the whole of humanity.*

God of all peoples?

I have other sheep that do not belong to this fold. I must bring them also, and they will listen to my voice. So there will be one flock, one shepherd. (John 10:16 NRSV)

I dreamt
that I was sitting at table
in the kingdom of God.
I waved to friends I recognised,
then looked to see who else was there.
Earthly distinctions were already beginning to fade
and it was clear
that the divided church
was divided no longer.

But that was only the beginning.
I turned to my neighbour
and found myself conversing
with a Muslim,
who said how pleased he was to see me there,
because he had always understood that Christians
were arrogant, aggressive,
and unwilling to listen to others.
I broke off
only to exchange jokes with a Hindu
and found myself wondering
who next I should meet...

Of course,
it was only a dream.

> I rejoice, Lord, that I can truly say,
> 'The Lord is my shepherd'
> but let me never forget
> that you also have other sheep
> and that your loving care
> is great enough to comprehend us all.

Living, we must learn to live

O crucified and risen Lord
destroy the bonds that bind us tight,
release us from our greed and pride
and lead your people into light.
> Born, we must be reborn,
> living, we must learn to live.

From dawdling by an empty tomb,
from eyes that look and fail to see,
from fear of death and fear of life
Lord set your foolish people free.

From thinking heaven's far away,
from fearing change and fearing strife,
from clinging to a world that's past
Lord, lead your people into life.

O triumph, found beyond defeat,
O good, we dream in evil days,
O love, no hatred could destroy,
possess our lives and shape our ways.

O crucified and risen Lord
you are the life, the truth, the way,
let Easter dawn blaze on our souls
and make us children of the day.
> Born, we must be reborn,
> living, we must learn to live.

Wider Horizons

Chapter 10

The End is the Beginning

For this perishable body must put on imperishability, and this mortal body must put on immortality. When this perishable body puts on imperishability, and this mortal body puts on immortality, then the saying that is written will be fulfilled:
  Death has been swallowed up in victory.
(1 Corinthians 15:53,54 NRSV)

- The inescapable fact of death

- Whence comes the dream?

- The four horsemen of the Apocalypse

- But if not... !

- Is heaven really out there?

- Plenty of accommodation!

- Judgement

- The reality of Hell

- The Saviour

- A light beyond the darkness

The inescapable fact of death

O Grave, where is thy victory?
O Death, where is thy sting?
thy victory is everywhere,
thy sting's in ev'rything.'

So wrote Studdert Kennedy, in 'Missing – Believed Killed', and those words speak as much for the anguish felt by many today as they try to come to terms with the death of a loved one, as they did for those bereaved by the carnage on the Western Front in the 1914-18 war.

Violence and death!
Stock subjects
for film, television and pulp fiction.
Stock subjects for our entertainment!

But death is real,
non reversible;
and real lives are all too often
needlessly and brutally
cut short.
Even when death comes naturally,
it leaves a painful legacy
of grief and loss.

The Gospel –
the 'Good News' –
starts with a gruesome death
proclaiming that it was not an end,
but a new beginning;
proclaiming that death is but a gateway
into a new dimension of life,
and challenging us to consider
what that new dimension implies.

Blessed be the God and Father of our Lord Jesus Christ!
By his great mercy he has given us a new birth into a living hope
through the resurrection of Jesus Christ from the dead.
(1 Peter 1:3 NRSV)

The End is the Beginning

O Lord of the kingdom
where losing is winning
and love has a strength which
gives promise of dawn;
teach us in our doubting
to know resurrection
and live in your world as
a people reborn.

O joy of the sinner
and hope of the dying,
O peace of the troubled
Lord, help us we pray;
banish now the sorrow,
the death which enfolds us,
forgive us, renew us,
restore us today.

O living Lord Jesus
we share in your triumph,
the world may be dark, but
we live by your word;
death has no dominion
for Jesus is risen
away with our grieving,
rejoice in the Lord.

O Lord in your kingdom
the poorest is welcome,
the homeless find lodging,
the outcast belong;
fill us with your loving
and free us Lord Jesus
to worship and serve you
all ages along.

The End is the Beginning

Whence comes the dream?

And I saw a new heaven and a new earth: for the first heaven and the first earth were passed away ... And I heard a great voice out of heaven saying, Behold, the tabernacle of God is with men, and he will dwell with them, and they shall be his people, and God himself shall be with them and be their God. And God shall wipe away all tears from their eyes; and there shall be no more death, neither sorrow, nor crying, neither shall there be any more pain; for the former things are passed away'.

(Revelation 21:1-4 AV)

Where does it come from,
the dream –
older than the scriptures,
older than recorded history –
the dream of something other,
something better,
something enduring,
something awaiting us,
involving us, challenging us;
something lying beyond the apparent finality of death?

Could such a universal reaching out to the unknown,
such a widespread belief
found in so many and diverse cultures
be conceivable,
were it not a response
to a desire,
a longing,
first planted
in the human heart
by the Creator of all that is?

> *You have made us for yourself
> and our hearts are restless
> until they rest in you.*
>
> Augustine of Hippo

The four horsemen of the Apocalypse

... they were given authority ... to kill with the sword, famine and pestilence, and by the wild animals of the earth. (Revelation 6:8 NRSV)

War, famine, pestilence and death;
the four horsemen
still ride through the earth,
setting nation against nation,
community against community,
neighbour against neighbour.

What hope can there be
for those who seek to bring
justice in place of anarchy,
to build,
to heal,
to be messengers of peace?
What sacrifices will they be called to make
and to what end?

Yet the horsemen's power is not unbounded.
The final word lies
not with the horsemen,
but with the God
who in Christ
suffers with those who suffer,
dies with those who die,
and reaches out lovingly and powerfully
that they may share in his resurrection.

When you hear of wars and rumours of wars, do not be alarmed; this must take place, but the end is still to come. For nation will rise against nation, and kingdom against kingdom; there will be earthquakes in various places; there will be famines. This is but the beginning of the birth pangs. (Mark 13:7-8 NRSV)

But if not...!

If our God whom we serve is able to deliver us from the furnace of blazing fire and out of your hand, O king, let him deliver us. But if not, be it known to you, O king, that we will not serve your gods and we will not worship the golden statue that you have set up.
(Daniel 3:17-18 NRSV)

But if not...!
These are pivotal words
in the story
of the three men cast into a blazing furnace.

Through those prepared to stand
against tyranny
and the worship of debased values;
through those who refuse to bow
before the prevailing wind
though their stand
may cost their life;
society is redeemed,
and God is glorified.

The story in Daniel finds it climax in a miraculous deliverance... But I see four men unbound, walking in the middle of the fire, and they are not hurt; and the fourth has the appearance of a god.
(Daniel 3:25 NRSV)

The account of Faithful's death in Vanity Fair sees God at work in a different way... Therefore he was presently condemned to be had from the place where he was, to the place from whence he came, and there to be put to the most cruel death that could be invented ... Thus came Faithful to his end ... Now I saw, that there stood behind the multitude a chariot and a couple of horses waiting for Faithful who, so soon as his adversaries had dispatched him, was taken up into it, and straightway was carried up through the clouds with sound of trumpet, the nearest way to the celestial gate.
(John Bunyan 'The Pilgrim's Progress')

The End is the Beginning

For all men and women
who have held fast to their faith
in the face of persecution and painful death:
for those whose names
are recorded and honoured
as saints and martyrs:
for that great host,
of many nations and languages
by name unknown to us,
but to you, both known and dear:
for these
and for all your faithful witnesses,
glory be to you
our Lord and Saviour.

From earth's wide bounds, from ocean's farthest coast,
through gates of pearl streams in the countless host,
singing to Father, Son and Holy Ghost:
Alleluia!

William Walsham How

Is heaven really out there?

Our Father, which art in Heaven,
hallowed be thy name... (Matthew 6:9. Luke 11:2 AV)

O Lord, you have searched me and known me. You know when I sit down and when I rise up; you discern my thoughts from far away. You search out my path and my lying down, and are acquainted with all my ways. (Psalm 139:1-3 NRSV)

If heaven were to be 'out there'
in a continually expanding universe
then age by age heaven would become ever more remote.

But heaven is the realm of the God
who is never far from any one of us,
so heaven cannot be remote;
even in the here and now
we may glimpse something of heaven,
something of the eternal kingdom.

God is love,
indestructible love,
which does not batten on
or smother the beloved,
but liberates,
that the beloved may bloom and mature.

Thus to enter heaven,
to pass from death to life,
must surely be to experience the joy
of broken relationships restored
and new relationships established,
as we find ourselves welcomed
into the kingdom where love is all in all.

> *Be near me, Lord Jesus; I ask thee to stay*
> *close by me for ever, and love me, I pray.*
> *Bless all the dear children in thy tender care*
> *and fit us for heaven to live with thee there. Anon.*

Plenty of accommodation !

In my Father's house are many mansions (AV) ... many dwelling places (NRSV) ... There are many rooms in my Father's house. (GNB)
(John 14:2)

'Go out at once into the streets and lanes of the town and bring in the poor, the crippled, the blind and the lame.' And the slave said, 'Sir, what you ordered has been done, and there is still room.'
(Luke 14:21,22 NRSV)

Many mansions,
plenty of accommodation,
room for all!

Jesus speaks to the fears
and apprehension of his friends
during their last supper together.
He is going home, he tells them,
back to the Father's house
where in due time
they will also find places prepared for them.

But his words were not just for those
gathered that night in an Upper Room.
From all points of the compass,
whatever their language, their nation,
or the colour of their skin;
men and women,
and particularly the poor,
the outcast,
the disadvantaged
and the lost,
will come and will find welcome
in the kingdom of God.

I am the bread of life. Whoever comes to me will never be hungry, and whoever believes in me will never be thirsty ... and anyone who comes to me I will never turn away. (John 6:35,37 REB)

Judgement

*You have come to Mount Zion and to the city of the living God ....
and to God the judge of all.* (Hebrews 12:22,23 NRSV)

*But who can endure the day of his coming, and who can stand when
he appears? For he is like a refiner's fire.* (Malachi 3:2 NRSV)

The moment had arrived.
Strangely calm, and comfortably seated,
I was waiting to enter the judgement hall,
wondering what, out of the patchwork of my living,
I might be able to offer
that could bear the scrutiny of God..

Then, suddenly,
I found my whole life unfolding before me;
I was not merely watching,
I was experiencing again its sorrows, its joys,
everything:
but with a deeper intensity of feeling
than I had ever known on earth.

Then came the pain.
I was facing occasions I would rather have forgotten.
Had I really been so blind,
so unfeeling,
so absorbed in myself,
so cruel?
Had I really wasted so many opportunities,
followed so many wrong paths?

All was still again,

but now I knew there was nothing I could say except –

    'God be merciful to me, a sinner'.

The reality of Hell

C S Lewis, in 'The Great Divorce', pictured hell as a place where anybody could have whatever they wished merely by thinking of it. There was even a bus to heaven if they wanted to go. But because anybody could have whatever they wished whenever they wanted, hell was full of empty houses, as people were continually moving ever further out to get away from their neighbours.

Modern, sophisticated people that we are,
can we really believe in hell?

If a soul should become so isolated within itself
that no spark of generosity,
no flicker of compassion,
no glimmer of love
is left;
that soul is surely already in hell.
It has cut itself off
from anything that might let in
the light of God's presence.

Whether any soul can resist the saving love of God
to all eternity
I wouldn't pretend to know;
but I do know
that the appeal of the Christian Way
is not the fear of hell,
but love and longing
for all that we see of God in Jesus Christ.

> *Then why, O blessed Jesus Christ*
> *should I not love thee well?*
> *Not for the sake of winning heaven,*
> *or of escaping hell;*
> *not with the hope of gaining aught;*
> *not seeking a reward;*
> *but as thyself has loved me,*
> *O ever-loving Lord*
>
> (16th Century, Translation Edward Caswell)

The Saviour

Truly, I tell you, today you will be with me in Paradise.
(Luke 23:43 NRSV)

Just one more terrorist –
or freedom fighter
according to your point of view –
He had probably killed
and killed again.
Now painfully he turns his eyes towards
the man crucified beside him,
and says,
'Jesus, remember me
when you come into your kingdom'.

Gloriously, the love of God
reaches out to the deserving poor,
the disadvantaged,
to all who have had a raw deal in life,
but, this man?
What could he expect by way of reply?

Is it shocking that he should hear,
'Today you will be with me in Paradise.'
or should we find it encouraging?

For us those words are a reminder
that It will not be our merit
that brings us to the kingdom,
but the love of Christ
which sets no limits
and holds nothing back.

Thanks be to God.

Shortly before he died after a long and eventful life John Newton said to a visitor, 'My memory is nearly gone; but I remember two things: that I am a great sinner, and that Christ is a great saviour.'

A Light beyond the darkness

A light beyond the darkness
a joy beyond the pain,
a youth beyond the aging,
a Lord who lives again :
> And dying isn't death,
> and failing isn't vain,
> the end is the beginning
> with the Lord who lives again!

A universe of wonder,
and thought beyond the brain,
a love beyond the hating
a Lord who lives again :
> And dying isn't death,
> and failing isn't vain,
> the end is the beginning
> with the Lord who lives again!

A health beyond the sickness
release from stress and strain,
a life beyond the dying
a Lord who lives again
> And dying isn't death,
> and failing isn't vain,
> the end is the beginning
> with the Lord who lives again!

From the play 'One Friday in Eternity'.

The End is the Beginning

Acknowledgements

From *The Maker of Things a light hearted cantata about our place in Creation* © Edmund Banyard. Published by Christian Education/Radius:

> *Before the Beginning*
> *And the Lord God Listened*
> *Holy is the Soil*

From the play *One Friday in Eternity* and/or the musical *One Friday* ©1972 Stainer and Bell:

> *Have you ever been lost?*
> *When the springs of my life*
> *One Friday in eternity*
> *It is accomplished*
> *A press conference*
> *A light beyond darkness.*

Angelo's Song from *The Flame* © Edmund Banyard published by Christian Education/Radius

Then and Us from *A Fistful of Fivers* © Edmund Banyard published by Christian Education/Radius

The Eternal Adam from *Adam* published in *Three One Act Plays* © Edmund Banyard published by BCC/Radius

From *Turn But a Stone* © 1992 Edmund Banyard published by Christian Education:

> *O crucified and risen Lord*
> *O Lord of the Kingdom*
> *When the springs of my life run dry*

Acknowledgments

Biblical Quotations:

The Good News Bible second edition © American Bible Society 1994. Used by permission.

The New Revised Standard Version © 1989 The Division of Christian Education of the National Council of the Churches of Christ in the United States of America. Used by permission.

The New Jerusalem Bible ©1985 Darton Longman and Todd Ltd. Used by permission.

The Revised English Bible © Oxford University Press and Cambridge University Press 1989. Used by permission.